Here's what I think...

A *born-again* *Yooper* speaks out

Selected Columns
By

Jerry Harju

"You'll be laughing long after you put the book down."
Green Bay Press Gazette

Here's what I think...

A born-again Yooper speaks out

by Jerry Harju

Cover Design by Stacey Willey

Editing by Karen Murr and Pat Green

Artwork by Bill Swanberg

Copyright 2000
Jerry Harju

Published by North Harbor Publishing
Marquette, Michigan

Publishing Coordination by
Globe Printing, Inc.
Ishpeming, Michigan

Printed by Sheridan Books, Chelsea, Michigan

ISBN 0-9670205-6-5
Library of Congress Card No. 00-103355

July 2000

INTRODUCTION

Forty-five years after I'd left Upper Michigan in 1951 for college and then on to sunny Southern California, I found my way back to God's country, this time for good. As usual, my timing was absolutely perfect; the winter of '96-'97 in the U.P. was one of the snowiest on record. While scraping ice and snow from my poor, shivering California car, it dawned on me that I had the makings of an amusing essay—a born-again Yooper becoming reacquainted with U.P. winters. I wrote it up and turned it in to the *Mining Journal,* the local Marquette newspaper. They liked the idea and printed it, the first of a long series of columns in that newspaper.

This book is a compilation of these columns. Some are my reactions to life's frustrating little encounters—dealing with telemarketers, computers, shopping at the supermarket, buying houses, etc. Others are reflections on the vast differences between living in the U.P. (a wonderful place) and Southern California (maybe a little less than wonderful). You'll also find many of my 1940's U.P. boyhood adventures, often wacky, always nostalgic. I hope you'll enjoy them. In any case, drop me a line. I'd like to hear from you.

Jerry Harju
528 E. Arch St.
Marquette, MI 49855
e-mail: jharju@bresnanlink.net

DEDICATION

To my two editors, Pat Green and Karen Murr,
who deserve more credit.

ACKNOWLEDGEMENTS

My sincere appreciation to Bruce Heisel, former editor of the *Mining Journal*, for giving me my big break as a newspaper columnist. Many thanks to the current *Mining Journal* staff—Dianne Biery, Dave Schneider, and Dan Weingarten for printing my colums over the years. My long-time editors, Pat Green and Karen Murr, have as usual, added immense quality to my prose, and thanks also to Jeff Jacobs, my U.P. technical advisor. Bill Swanberg provided a clever drawing of yours truly, and Stacey Willey of Globe Printing did a very skillful job on the cover design and page layout, using computer software that I don't understand at all.

Other Books by Jerry Harju

Northern Reflections
Northern D'Lights
Northern Passages
The Class of '57
Cold Cash

TABLE OF CONTENTS

HOW COULD I FORGET U.P. WINTERS?

Three months ago I moved from sunny, palm-tree-studded Marina del Rey, California, to Marquette, Michigan. Why would anyone want to do a dumb thing like that, many Yoopers asked me. Why move indeed—especially at the onset of winter—from a climate where people bundle up when the wind chill dips to sixty above zero to a place where in January you need a metal detector to find your mailbox.

Needless to say, having spent my early years in Marquette County before leaving for college in 1951, I should remember U.P. winters. Yet after forty-six years, I had forgotten.

Cars, for example. I'd forgotten how snowdrifts form on the engine block of a car left outside in a blizzard, even with the hood closed. Ignition systems really hate snowdrifts.

Fortunately, as soon as I arrived, I was advised to buy a really *big* car battery. In California, guys brag about engine horsepower. Winter-hardened Yoopers don't concern themselves with horsepower; it's the *battery* that counts.

The day I was at Willey's in Ishpeming, buying my battery, another battery customer asked me, "How big a one did'ja buy?"

"Eight hundred and fifty cranking amps," I proudly replied. The week before, I'd never heard of cranking amps, but I'd successfully picked up on Yooper battery jargon and ordered the biggest one in stock.

He nodded but wasn't impressed. "I hear they'll be making 'em with a thousand amps pretty soon. I'm gonna get one of those."

I'd forgotten how any car mechanism with small moving parts will freeze up in the winter. Everyone knows about door locks, and of course I promptly had mine frozen solid. My Oldsmobile also has an electric radio antenna that cleverly slides down into the fender when the ignition is turned off. Don't buy a car with one of these. Electric radio antennas are made in tropical third-world countries by people who've never seen water freeze. In cold weather the antennas automatically sense that the inside of the fender is much cozier than the frigid outside air and refuse to come out.

I'd also forgotten that it's impossible to keep a car clean during a U.P. winter. In California I faithfully took my Oldsmobile to the car wash every week. Up here there are mammoth four-wheel-drive vehicles lurking around car washes, waiting with engines running for you to exit the car wash with your sparkling-clean automobile. They're ready for you. As soon as you get on the highway, they pass at high speed, grillwork grinning fiendishly as their snow tires churn up that delightfully gooey mixture of snow, sand, and salt so unique to the U.P. Your beautiful automobile instantly turns into a large chocolate cupcake.

Of course, with winter in full swing it's hard to tell if the car is dirty or not because it's been totally encrusted with ice and snow ever since the first weekly blizzard. Every morning I spend fifteen or twenty minutes chipping away at the ice and snow, removing just enough to see where I'm going. Months ago, Jeff Jacobs, my friend in Ishpeming, told me that his new Jeep Cherokee came with defrosters on the side mirrors. "That's the most ridiculous thing I ever heard of!" I cried. "Why waste good money on stupid gadgets like mirror defrosters?" Now I'm wondering if I can get them installed on my Olds.

I'd forgotten about icicles, too. My apartment on the edge of south Marquette has a beautiful view of the woods, but after the first snow, icicles began hanging from the eaves. I mean, these were not just your run-of-the-mill icicles; these were major-league icicles growing three or four feet a day. In no time at all the wonderful view—not to mention the daylight—was being obscured, so I hustled over to Wal-Mart and bought a long-handled windshield scraper to knock the icicles off.

But I'd waited too long. Many of the icicles were now as big as tree trunks, and they just scoffed at my plastic scraper. I've since bought a no-nonsense steel-bladed shovel and now attack the icicles every day while they're still puppy size.

In my years in Southern California, I never got a grocery shopping cart stuck in the snow, but the other day, in the Econo Foods parking lot, I did just that trying to wheel my weekly food supply to the car. You forget things like that happen up here.

But in true Yooper fashion, I'm adapting. I've got the right equipment now—heavy jacket, Sorel boots, mitts with liners, ski mask, shovels, spray deicer, windshield scraper, and snow brush. Except for one thing: I'm thinking about getting a BOSS snowplow if I can find a light blue one to match the Oldsmobile.

So why did I move here from California? It's simple, really. My ninety-five-year-old mother smiles every time I visit her at the nursing home in Ishpeming. If my apartment building shakes, it's comforting to know that it's only the weekly blizzard coming off Lake Superior and not *The Big One*. And when holes begin to appear in the Oldsmobile I'll know it's only road salt—not bullets.

❂ ❂ ❂

CRIME DOESN'T PAY IN THE U.P.

When I was living in Los Angeles I regularly watched the early morning news on television, because with L.A.'s four seasons—fire, flood, mud slides, and riots—it was always wise to check to see if it's safe to go outside.

But it was the L.A. urban crime news that really depressed me. Every morning it took newscasters ten minutes simply to wade through yesterday's murders—and those were the ones committed by the *celebrities.* If you were a nobody, you didn't even get mentioned.

Consequently, one of the reasons I moved to Marquette last November is the low crime rate in the U.P. Even though Upper Michigan people are concerned about the increase in crime, there's still a lot less of it here than in the big cities. The reason is that criminals need anonymity to succeed.

Take bank robbery, for instance. In Los Angeles robbing banks has become an art form, surpassing sun bathing in popularity. Any bozo can take a gun into a bank, grab the cash from a teller who's never seen him before, get in his car, and make his getaway into the thousand-mile labyrinth of freeways. He stands an excellent chance of never being caught because there's millions of people out there—very few who know him. He merely submerges into the ocean of humanity.

That's hard to do up here. Remember back in 1994 when a bank in one of our small towns got robbed? The would-be robber—a local boy—parked his car, put on a ski mask, grabbed a shotgun, and walked into the bank. Three women—all of whom knew him *and* his car—were having coffee in the restaurant across the street and were watching the whole thing through the front window.

The robber came out of the bank with his shotgun and a bag of cash, only to be confronted by a fourth woman who, likely as not, went to church with his mother. Totally irate, she began chasing him—probably intent on giving him a good whacking—finally driving him into a nearby swamp.

The police quickly arrived and interviewed all the witnesses to the crime. When they asked for a description of the robber they promptly received it. One of the women asked, "Would you like his name, too?" The suspect was picked up thirty minutes later.

One could argue that since the bank robber was so well known in that town, he should have gone to Ishpeming or somewhere else to pull the job. It wouldn't have made any difference—someone in Ishpeming would have undoubtedly recognized him, too. There just aren't that many people up here. Everyone knows or is related to everyone else.

Another reason for our lower crime rate is that for even less-serious offenses you can suffer stiff social penalties in addition to what the courts hand out. For example, suppose you've had one too many and run your car off the road. If it's a slow news day—and it often is—the local television station—cameras pointing and grinding—will swoop down on the accident scene like an eagle after a rabbit. Everyone in the county will be viewing your slack-jawed, bleary-eyed face on the six o'clock news.

"Arvid, come over here and look who they got on the news . . . will you look at those bloodshot eyes? I wonder if his wife knows he was over in Palmer. I'll bet he was drinking with those deer-hunting cronies of his. I think I'll give her a call."

And when you get in trouble with the law up here, the news reporting includes *everything*. Picture what might happen if your wife decides to apply vigilante justice to your drunken misdemeanor.

"Hello?"

"Hi, Florence, this is Beatrice. Did you see in today's paper where Helmi got arrested? Her husband came home drunk with the car banged up, and she grabbed his 30-30 and shot him in the leg."

"I read it. He deserves it, the bum. But did you see what they put down as her *age*? *SIXTY-ONE*! All these years she's been telling everybody that she's five years younger than me—wait'll I tell Gladys . . . "

So for those of you who are thinking of a life of crime in the U.P., I recommend you go down to Green Bay, Milwaukee, or another one of those big places. You'll have better luck. Even if you're caught, there'll be more respect for your privacy.

SPRING FLINGS IN A MODEL A

Springtime has finally arrived in the U.P.—the signs are everywhere: long-buried mail boxes and street signs have popped their heads above the dwindling earthen-colored snowbanks; floodwaters are gently lapping at riverfront doorsteps; potholes are in full bloom. And of course, in the spring a young man's fancy turns to thoughts of love.

When I was young I too had springtime thoughts of love, but only after I'd completed one vital task: getting my car started.

During my high-school years in Republic, I was the proud owner of a 1930 Model A Ford, enabling me to seriously compete with the other young bucks in our never-ending quest for girls. Without that car I would have been a lonely, unloved pedestrian, spurned by all womankind.

I couldn't afford new parts for the Model A because all my money went for gasoline—at eighteen cents a gallon, a major drain on my finances. Consequently, everything on that old Ford—the battery, tires, generator, and fan belt—was in terrible shape. The car typically refused to run in cold weather, so every winter I put it up on blocks in the backyard with the tires stored in the woodshed and the battery in the house.

But as soon as the temperature began hovering consistently in the thirties, I rejoiced, officially declaring it springtime. I rushed to the backyard to take the Model A out of hibernation.

In the woodshed, I'd pull the inner tubes out of the tires, inflate the tubes with a hand pump, and take them into the kitchen to be dunked in a sink full of water. Air bubbles indicated leaks to be patched (there were always several). I'd stocked up on inner-tube patches—another major but necessary expense—which had an inflammable substance on one side and a rubber compound on the other. The patch was placed, rubber side down, over the hole in the tube and the inflammable side was lit with a kitchen match. With a large puff of vile-smelling smoke—my mother really hated this—the patch vulcanized itself to the inner tube.

The tire frequently required a boot—a large piece of plied rubber inserted in the tire—to shield the inner tube from a hole in the tread or sidewall. Boots made the tires enormously unbalanced, and going over forty-five miles an hour was asking for trouble akin to passing through the sound barrier.

Next came the carburetor. It only had about six moving parts, and even a mechanically challenged person like myself could completely disassemble it, lovingly bathe each piece in gasoline, and put it back together again.

Finally, I took the battery from its winter resting place under my bed and carried it over to the Standard service station for a luxurious, overnight seventy-five-cent slow charge.

The moment of truth arrived: time to start up the car. The engine had to be turned over a few times with the hand crank (standard equipment on a Model A) to prime the carburetor and arouse the long-slumbering motor oil. Then I'd get behind the wheel, turn on the ignition, adjust the spark advance, pull out the choke knob, utter a few prayers, and punch the electric starter button with my foot. If everything was done right—and this never happened the first time—the four-cylinder engine would spring to life with a throaty BUCKETA-BUCKETA-BUCKETA.

I'd feverishly put the Model A in gear and roar off down the gravel road to begin the courtship ritual of cruising endlessly around downtown Republic. The girls, no doubt, got an immediate thrill when they first heard the familiar FLUMP-FLUMP-FLUMP-FLUMP of the boots in my severely unbalanced tires. They knew that spring had arrived and love was in the air.

These days I can still turn my fancy to thoughts of love with the best of 'em. In fact, I recently flew to Los Angeles for a springtime rendezvous with my lady friend Pat.

I don't drive at all on our dates out there—she chauffeurs me around in a late-model Chevrolet which she keeps running all winter long. The Chevy's tires are in excellent shape and don't even have inner tubes. The battery never goes dead. The carburetor has been replaced by an electronically controlled fuel injection system which I wouldn't even be able to *find*, much less clean.

I should have put a boot into one of the Chevy's tires when we drove over to our favorite restaurant for a romantic candlelight dinner. The FLUMP-FLUMP-FLUMP-FLUMP would have been a nice touch.

A NORTH-POLE JUNKIE HANGS UP ANOTHER SEASON

Don't laugh now, but some months ago I attempted to reach the North Pole. I'm not kidding. And this is the third time I've gone on this wacky trip. First, a little background.

The North Pole is located in the middle of the Arctic Ocean on an extensive floating icecap that expands and contracts with the seasons. It's in total darkness for much of the year, but by April, daylight lasts for twenty-four-hours, continuing throughout the summer. If you're inclined to travel to the North Pole, April is the best month, given the constant daylight and relatively stable weather that's cold enough (twenty below zero Fahrenheit) to keep the ice firm.

But it's no trip to Disneyland. Besides the brutal cold, there are other problems. Pressure ridges formed from buckling ice can reach heights of thirty feet or more and must be climbed over with heavy loads of equipment and supplies. Open channels of water lie across your path, stretching for long distances. They have to be either crossed—very tricky and dangerous—or skirted around, adding many miles to the journey. Finally, the ice itself frequently drifts southward. You can walk fifteen miles a day toward the Pole and drift back ten. But making the trip on foot is for certifiable lunatics. I travel by air.

Five years ago I paid a large sum of money to an arctic exploration outfit to fly me to the North Pole and land on the ice in a small plane outfitted with skis. At the time it sounded like a painless way to stand on the Pole, hold up a flag, get my picture taken wearing a sappy grin, and later be able to say that *I DID IT*!

It didn't work out as planned. The pilot of the small Twin Otter plane circled the Pole at very low altitude, but a thick bank of fog went right down to the polar ice and we couldn't land. I chalked up the venture as a ridiculous middle-aged attempt to recapture my youth and went back to my sane, mundane, paper-shuffling, workaday world.

But I'd become friends with the owner of the exploration company and one night in April '94 he called me.

"Wanna go on a North Pole trip?" he asked.

"I tried that, remember? Are you falling behind on your house payments again and need some quick cash?"

"This time it's free."

"Free?"

"Yep. I can't make the trip this year and I need a group leader."

The polar-expedition group leader meets with the paying clients at the beginning of the excursion, inspects their clothing so they won't charge out into the frozen tundra wearing leather dress gloves instead of wool-lined mitts, explains that polar bears, not humans, are at the top of the arctic food chain, and then shepherds them from one stopover point to the next. Unfortunately, the group leader's job description doesn't actually include *going* to the North Pole. The final 690-mile leg from Eureka—a Canadian weather station on the eightieth parallel— to the Pole required that the plane carry such a huge load of fuel that the group leader is considered extraneous weight.

However, many of the clients come from warm climates, and if even one of them chickened out at the last minute after experiencing the first taste of a minus-sixty-degree wind chill, it would lighten the plane and I'd have another shot.

"When do I leave?" I asked.

But all the clients hung in there, and on the day they travelled to the Pole I waited for their return at the weather station, passing time by throwing food scraps to the white arctic foxes that came begging at the kitchen door.

This past April I got another call.

"I've only got four clients this year—plenty of room for the group leader to ride all the way to the Pole. Interested?"

"When do I leave?" I asked.

I met the four men at Edmonton, Alberta, and we headed north, making stops at high arctic Inuit (Eskimo) villages before winding up at the Eureka weather station on 21 April.

Even *flying* to the Pole isn't without its problems. The Twin Otter doesn't have enough range to make the final leg nonstop, so the small arctic airline company deposits drums of fuel on the icecap at around the 87th parallel, 200 miles from the Pole. It's an unmanned, self-service gas station, if you will. The strategy is to put the plane down on the icecap at this unmanned fuel cache, refuel, and continue on to the Pole.

But refuelling can be tricky. To land anywhere on the icecap, conditions have to be near perfect. An overcast sky can produce flat light, preventing the pilot from using shadows to distinguish any roughness in the ice that could damage the landing gear, or worse, crack up the airplane. This is *not* the place to have an accident.

But the morning of the twenty-second was bright and clear, and the adrenalin was running high as we took off from the Eureka airstrip on the 1380-mile round trip flight to the North Pole. It looked good.

Good, that is, until we got about twenty miles south of the fuel cache where thick cloud cover shut off the sunlight, producing a flat-light condition.

But the fuel cache site had been used several times recently and the pilot knew that the ice had been pretty smooth. After circling around the drums at low altitude for one last inspection, he brought the plane in for a landing.

The Otter hit the ice like a barrel of bricks. It began pitching and rolling crazily as it skittered and banged along the icecap. Ten seconds later we finally bounced to a stop. After thousands of airplane landings, I suddenly realized the value of a seat belt—it keeps you from bouncing off the walls of the airplane.

A polar storm a few days earlier had blown snow across the marked landing area at the fuel cache, forming two-foot-high drifts that were virtually invisible from the air, especially in flat light. Extreme cold had hardened the drifts so that the Otter's landing skis bounced off rather than going through them.

The pilot stepped out of his cockpit door and grabbed a shovel from the plane's luggage compartment, dourly motioning for us to get out of the plane.

"The first order of business is to clear a strip so we can get this plane off the ice again," he said soberly. He stared out into the icy wind, the direction he wanted to take off into, and with the shovel quickly began to chop the nearest snow drift into chunks like he was going to build an igloo.

"How long a strip do you need?" I asked him.

"Five hundred feet."

Five hundred feet is nothing at an airport, but five hundred feet on a polar icecap filled with hardened snow drifts that must be removed was a long, long way.

With the pilot carving up the snow into chunks, the rest of us diligently followed along behind, furiously throwing or carrying the pieces off to one side. The wind chill factor was a bracing thirty-five below zero, and this fact alone made the runway construction very efficient. If we'd stopped to take a break, we would have frozen.

"Are you going to refuel when we get this done?" I asked the pilot.

"I don't think it's a good idea. With a full load of fuel, we'd need almost a thousand feet to get the plane in the air."

I looked at the runway we were laboring on, perhaps two hundred feet cleared and *that* didn't look all that great. The construction crew—myself; Amy, the lady copilot from Ontario; a plant nursery-store owner from Long Island; a missile engineer from Alabama; a psychiatrist from Nashville; and a system analyst from Baltimore—was beginning to stagger from exhaustion.

"Five hundred feet it is," I said licking at the icicles growing from my mustache.

After an hour and a half when we just about had the job done, the wind shifted ninety degrees.

"Taking off from this stuff in a crosswind is bad," the pilot said. "I think we'd better build another runway."

"How about a control tower while we're at it?" I suggested. No one laughed.

After three hours on the icecap we finished the second runway and scrambled into the plane before the wind changed its mind again. The pilot looked at the portly psychiatrist from Nashville. "Would you mind sitting in the rear of the cabin? I have to get the nose of the plane up quickly on takeoff."

With both engines screaming, the Otter bounced along our homemade runway and leapt into the air. We headed south. Without the extra fuel, we had to return to the Eureka weather station.

But our fortunes appeared to change that evening. A five-man British expedition walking to the Pole had made a distress radio call to Eureka. They needed a medical evacuation for one of their party. After several phone calls a cost-sharing plan between us and the British sponsors was agreed upon. However, the fuel cache site was now off limits due to the dangerous landing conditions, and the plan was to load as many 55-gallon fuel drums into the Otter as possible, fly to the North Pole nonstop, refuel the plane from the drums upon landing, and pick up the British evacuee on the return trip.

The next morning our pilot came up to me in the Eureka dining room during breakfast. "With all those fuel drums aboard, I can only take four people maximum without exceeding the plane's payload capacity."

The four clients with me had paid several thousand dollars apiece to get to the North Pole. I had paid nothing, so there was no question who was the odd man out. So while the clients and pilots flew to the Pole on their dual mission, I again hung around the weather station.

After dinner I was still feeling morose when I looked out a window and spotted a white arctic wolf standing about twenty feet from the front door. I grabbed my camera and snapped his picture before he trotted off. My spirits lifted and I had to tell someone. John MacIver, one of the weather analysts I had gotten to know, was in the station's rec room sipping a glass of home-made beer that they brewed at the station during the long winter nights. I mentioned the wolf.

"Yeah, there's been a lot of 'em around here lately—pretty tame, too," he replied. "Every once in awhile a few of the guys tie a wiener on the end of some fishing line and cast it out onto the ice. Sometimes a wolf'll chase the wiener when you reel it back in." He chuckled. "It's a lot of fun, even the wolf enjoys it."

It was an outrageous story, and I didn't know whether to believe him or not. It could be true; people get a little strange after they've been up in the arctic awhile. I think *I'm* getting a little strange. I've been up there three times now and have yet to stand on the North Pole. But for some reason I keep coming back. Maybe it's flying over Ellsmere Island's majestically stark mountains covered with blue-white ice and snow, where no man has set foot and hopefully never will. Maybe it's the people who live and work up here, taking on the frightening elements with casualness, patience, and biting humor. Maybe it's the wolf, unconcernedly standing out by the front door, looking right at home because, after all, he *is* at home.

If I get a call next April, asking if I want to take another group up to the Pole, I'll say, "When do I leave?" I really don't expect too much anymore. It'll just be an all-expense-paid trip to the eightieth parallel. Maybe next time I'll take up fishing for wolves.

BRING BACK EXHAUST PORTS

Recently I took in the Eighth Annual Antique Automobile Exhibit at the Michigan Iron Industry Museum in Negaunee. I attended last year too, and there were many of the same cars with the same owners sitting under the same trees, swapping the same restoration stories. It was a lot of fun, though, and I'll be back next year.

There are always several Model A Fords at the show. This year, a couple of them were identical to the 1930 two-door sedan I owned in high school. One in particular was show-room perfect—gleaming black paint, new 4.75X19 tires, pristine mohair seat upholstery, napped cotton headliner, and a mirror-like finish on the chromed bumpers. Mine never looked like that. In fact, Henry Ford's *NEW* ones rolling off the assembly line never looked like that. It was standing unguarded with the keys in the ignition, and for a moment . . . oh well, it's too late now.

I take great delight in identifying old cars. The proud owners put signs by their autos to clue the spectators on the make and model, but I only use the signs for verification.

For example, recognizing a '37 Ford is easy with its magnificently large V-shaped wraparound grill and radical "new design" where the headlights melt right into the fenders. Any Buick from the fifties is child's play with its distinctive exhaust ports on each front fender. I can spot an old Hudson Hornet's beetle-shaped body a mile away.

Years ago, every auto maker took on an obligation to design cars with individual character. A Chevy looked markedly different from a Ford, Plymouth, or Studebaker. The manufacturers even made sure you could see the difference between the cars in their own line. You could never mistake the fun-loving, perky 1949 Ford for its more muscular but quietly elegant big brother, the 1949 Mercury—it was like night and day.

Many of these designs were radical. The 1950 Studebaker rear end was so much like the front end that you couldn't tell if it was coming or going. A 1951 Nash Ambassador resembled an upside-down bathtub. The 1958 Edsel—the infamous financial disaster for Ford—had an O-shaped grill that looked like an Oldsmobile sucking a lemon. But like 'em or not, every car had its own character, and its owner defended it to the hilt. Guys would sit around the local gas station and heatedly discuss the virtues of Pontiacs, DeSotos, Chryslers, and even Kaisers and Frasers (remember them?). There was fierce brand loyalty, and it had more to do with appearance than anything else.

But things changed over the years. In 1965 I was shopping around for a new car and found that I had trouble telling them apart. The exhaust ports on the Buicks had disappeared completely. The new Fords, Chevys, Plymouths, and all the rest had huge wraparound windshields with nine-yard-long hoods and trunk decks. The grills—once the hallmark of every car—had been reduced to mean-looking narrow slits that separated two pairs of headlights (Why would a car need four headlights?) I wound up buying a two-headlighted Chevy pickup truck.

And it's gotten worse. All of the auto designers are now turning out pregnant walruses, abandoning the use of straight, crisp lines completely. Everything—the hood, trunk, top, side panels—is curved.

Every white mid-size sedan looks like a giant scoop of vanilla ice cream on wheels. That's not any worse than the '51 Nash "bathtub" look, but now they're *ALL* doing it.

In 1991 I bought a used 1988 Oldsmobile—still driving it today—which at least has some sharp edges on it. Even so, I occasionally get it confused with the rest of the herd. A few months ago I climbed into an unlocked car in the Wal-Mart parking lot. It turned out to be someone else's Buick.

Make no mistake, cars are better than they were forty or fifty years ago. They're roomier, smoother riding, easier to steer, safer to stop, and get about twice the gas mileage as the old jalopies. And you stand a reasonable chance of driving from Marquette to Detroit without two flat tires and several radiator boilovers. I just wish they had a little personality. Give me something to drive that stands out from the millions of pastel-colored marshmallows rolling down the road today.

Let's tell General Motors to build a car using all of their latest mechanical technology—the economical V-6 engine, anti-lock brakes, power rack-and-pinion steering, MacPherson strut suspension, and air bags all around. Then slip a 1953 Buick Roadmaster body over it, complete with the big toothy grill and the four exhaust ports on each front fender. Now *that* would be a car.

GROCERY WARS

There are certain advantages to being a bachelor. I can watch the Cubs or White Sox on WGN every night without quarrelsome negotiations with someone who'd rather see "Cybill" or "Mad About You." I'm perfectly content to use place settings of paper plates and cups and plastic forks and spoons. No one complains if I have sardine sandwiches for dinner three nights a week.

But one downside to bachelorhood is grocery shopping. There's no wife around to ask me "What would you like for dinner this week, honey?" and then go off to the supermarket and buy the stuff. If I want those sardines, I have to get them myself.

I hate grocery shopping and try to get it done as quickly as possible, but there are many obstacles. First I enter the store and try to yank a cart loose from the stack of shopping carts. There must be little interlocking mechanisms on these carts designed by NASA engineers to keep the carts locked together like segments on a space station. Once I pry one loose, I discover that it has one wheel frozen sideways. There was no point in getting another cart; they're all built that way.

I frantically push the cart down miles of aisles in quest of my paper dinnerware, apples, bananas, Grapenuts, milk, yogurt, and sardines. I can do this very fast once I learn my way around the store, but of course, store managers realize this and move everything around from time to time to keep me off balance.

The supermarket also puts other hindrances in my path. Did you ever notice that the milk cartons standing right inside the cooler door have an expiration date of today? Grocery clerks are trained to put the fresh milk way in the back. I flirt with shoulder dislocation every time I stick my arm in there some four feet, trying to grab a carton of milk that will survive a week.

I eat a lot of bananas. There are generally only two kinds of bananas in supermarkets: unripe ones—so green that you could pound ten-penny nails with them—and the ripe ones, which will turn to mush on the way home and piddle all over the car seat. Where are the in-between bananas?

Many people consider grocery shopping a social experience. I'll be careening around the end of an aisle—cart leaning over on two wheels, rubber burning—only to come charging up on two recipe-swappers standing in the middle of the next aisle. Shopping carts should come equipped with horns and power brakes.

Checkout lines are the worst. I study each one carefully, inspecting the people and the contents of their carts to determine which line would move the fastest. Married couples with small kids are to be avoided at all cost. They have a full basket, a wad of discount coupons, and always pay by check or credit card. I usually stand behind a lone man, figuring that he, like myself, is still using real money. This doesn't always work, though. Sometimes at the last minute his wife will come rushing up with an armload of food and begin writing out a check.

"Cash Only" lines are the best; they move fast. Although once, when I was living in California, I was standing in a "Cash Only" line when a woman ahead of me whipped out a checkbook to pay for her groceries. Being in my usual, surly supermarket mood, I barked, "This is cash only!" Several of the cash payers in line with me took up the cry, and a riot was in the making when the checkbook woman stopped us cold with, "You all can step up here and pay cash for my groceries if you like."

Shortly thereafter, recognizing my inability to cope with the high stress of supermarkets, I struck a deal with a woman I knew to do my weekly grocery shopping for a fee. This arrangement lasted for years. She couldn't believe her good luck, someone actually paying her to do such a pleasurable thing as shopping.

But you'll be happy to know I'm buying my own groceries again, and I'm mellowing out, partly because I'm now living in the stress-free U.P. and partly because I'm older and have risen above such immature behavior as running down slow-moving shoppers with my cart and yelling at people with checkbooks.

It also helps that I get to Econofoods at five in the morning. The only other person in the store is one sleepy graveyard-shift checkout person who is grateful for the break in the monotony when, after fifteen minutes of rushing up and down the aisles, I screech up to the register and dump the contents of my cart in front of her.

I still don't know what happens to those in-between bananas, though.

CONFESSIONS OF A GOLF JUNKIE

This may be the last column I'll write for some time, because I'm fighting a personal battle with an addiction I thought I'd conquered years ago. It may require counselling, or even checking into one of those fancy clinics they have out in the Southwest.

I've taken up golf again.

I began playing golf at the age of twelve. After World War II, my parents had live-in jobs at a large exclusive country club just outside Milwaukee. There were no other kids there, and I began hanging around the golf pro shop since there wasn't much else to do.

The golf pro—to keep me from getting underfoot—gave me a wooden-shaft mashie (a five iron to you youngsters) and some well-used golf balls and sent me over to a secluded grassy area to practice.

For weeks I hammered away at those golf balls, finally getting so I could get them up in the air pretty good. One evening I asked the pro if I could play the course before sundown when no one was around. After cautioning me to replace my divots and to take great care putting on the green with the mashie, he agreed to let me play, but only the 425-yard first hole, so he could keep an eye on me from the pro-shop window.

More weeks went by. Every evening I played that first hole over and over, holing out on the green and racing the 425 yards back to the tee to do it all over again. I became obsessed with golf.

Throughout my teen years, I worked summers at Milwaukee golf clubs, caddying, running the driving range, and working in the pro shop. By now I had a full complement of equipment—clubs, bag, golf shoes, and all the rest. I played a round of golf every day.

Along the way I discovered one thing. GOLF IS NOT FUN.

With most sports, you get better with practice. This is not true of golf. Your progress is monitored by the gods of golf. They allow you to achieve a certain level of proficiency and then, with fiendish delight, begin dinking with your game.

These gods occasionally permit you to have one good round of golf—long, straight drives, accurate iron shots, fabulous putts. Then they whisper in your ear that your scores could be even lower and your drives much longer if you'd put just a touch more muscle into your swing. This, of course, is pure baloney and from experience you know it, but you can't resist putting it to the test. Swinging harder usually results in a two-foot drive after you've ticked the top two microns of the ball.

In baseball, the pitcher tries to make the ball *curve*, and the baseball wants to go straight. The opposite is true with a golf ball. A golfer wants to hit the ball *straight*, but the golf ball—and this is where the gods of golf make it interesting—thinks otherwise. When struck, the ball swerves violently to the right or left, seeking nuisance terrain like high grass, dense woods, or deep standing water. The frequency of this occurring is directly proportional to the amount of practice and lessons you've taken.

Thankfully for me, fate intervened. During college I had little time to play, and afterward, while living in Los Angeles, it was necessary to take out a third mortgage to pay the greens fee on local golf courses. And once you teed off, it took most of the daylight hours to play eighteen holes because half the population of L.A. was hacking and cursing on the holes up ahead of you. Eventually I gave the game up. I'd finally kicked the habit.

Then, after many, happy golf-free years, I moved back to the U.P. The first thing I noticed was that the local courses—much greener and more scenic than the Los Angeles courses—had fewer people on them. I mentioned this to my friend, Jeff Jacobs, an avid golfer.

"It's also much cheaper to play here than in the big city," he added.

The next thing I knew, the two of us were out on a practice range hitting a bucket of balls using Jeff's clubs. "Just to get some fresh air and sunshine," I rationalized to myself, but I should have recognized the early symptoms: hitting the range balls faster and faster until they were all gone and then sneaking off the front of the practice tee, retrieving dubbed balls just to get in a few more shots.

One day Jeff brought over another set of clubs. "I had this spare set in my closet. You might as well keep them in the trunk of your car for when we go out to practice again."

I began going to practice ranges alone—another ominous sign— and then I took a lesson from Marc Gilmore, the pro at the Marquette Country Club.

"That's a good basic swing you have," he said tactfully. He made a few suggestions and—lo and behold—I began hitting five-iron shots ten yards further than when I was a teenager. Full of hope, I rushed down to Ishpeming to find Jeff. We got in nine holes at Wawonowin Country Club before sundown—the first round of golf I'd played in twenty years.

For some reason, the tips the pro gave me earlier didn't seem to work and Jeff beat me handily. But after a twenty-year layoff I BROKE SIXTY. Not only that, on a treacherous par three with a well-trapped, elevated green, I MADE PAR! The gods of golf smiled, nodded, and said to themselves, "He's back in the fold."

After twenty years of being clean, I've fallen off the golf wagon. Obviously, it's all Jeff Jacobs' fault. He knew I was a recovered golfoholic and still lured me out to the practice range and donated those clubs. I hold him entirely responsible, and as soon as I get rid of this damfool slice, I'm going to get him back out on the course and beat his butt.

A LITTLE ROAD WITH OUR POTHOLES, PLEASE

Early signs of autumn are everywhere in Upper Michigan—frosty mornings pinching your cheeks; leaves turning brilliant shades of reds and yellows; and the pungent fragrance of hot asphalt spicing the air as county workers man huge yellow backhoes, rollers, and front-end loaders frantically attempting to put the finishing touches to the summer's road-repair projects.

These workers are mending the crater-size potholes and frost heaves that always appear after the spring thaw. As usual, the county road commissions have correctly reasoned that there isn't enough asphalt on the planet to fill all the potholes in Upper Michigan, so they spend the early summer months determining which roads are in the worst shape. By the time all of the necessary road inspections are made and the ROAD-CLOSED-TO-THRU-TRAFFIC signs are touched up with fresh paint, August has arrived, leaving little time to do the actual work. Suddenly, every road worker and available piece of heavy equipment is called out and put into service.

At this time of year if you want to drive from Marquette to Iron Mountain, don't be in a hurry. The highway suddenly narrows to a single lane, and you'll cool your heels in a long line of vehicles that extends well beyond the curvature of the earth while hard-hatted flagpersons holding STOP signs engage in long chats with each other on walkie talkies. The trip will kill an afternoon.

Have you been to Negaunee lately? It's hard to tell if they're repairing the roads or starting up a new open-pit iron mine in the middle of town. There are more John Deeres and Caterpillars on the streets than Fords and Chevrolets.

The county road commissioners have made every effort to calm citizens' nerves by offering scenic detours. For example, Lakeshore Drive in Ishpeming has been transformed—temporarily, I trust—into the Sand and Gravel Mountain Range.

Repairing the roads is a high priority, and no one complains much about the inconvenience. However, I read a disturbing article in the *Mining Journal* the other day. It seems that city council members in Ishpeming and Negaunee are concerned because some of the pavement laid last year is already beginning to crumble—something about shale in the asphalt mixture retaining moisture that leads to cracking.

Pavement lasting one year? Is this a trend? Grove Street—my quickest route home from downtown Marquette—has been under repair all summer long and inaccessible to through traffic. Does this mean that next May—thanks to Jack Frost and his merry little asphalt pranks— the street will be back in the same shape as it was this spring and they'll close it down as soon as the snow melts? Will I only be able to drive on Grove Street in the winter?

I can see it all now. Before long *all* the roads in the U.P. will be under repair *every summer*. The city fathers of Negaunee, faced with financial crisis, will wash their hands of the whole matter and turn the responsibility over to homeowners. Negauneeites will be buying state-of-the-art backhoes and asphalt rollers and paving the street in front of their houses, competing with their neighbors for the nicest-looking and smoothest pavement on the block. The Marquette Chamber of Commerce will advertise walking trails to tourists—through town. NMU will offer advanced asphalt-laying degrees.

I'm in favor of a fresh approach. Take all the winter snow that we always have so much trouble getting rid of and store it in huge insulated warehouses. When summer arrives, spread the snow on the highways every day. It's gentler on the cars than potholes, much cheaper than asphalt, and keeps your winter driving skills sharp. We could sell the road-repair equipment to Lower Michigan. I think this has definite potential.

WHAT THE #*!*?* IS WITH TV?

I was channel surfing the other night and came across one of the major network's new fall offerings: a cops and robbers program. Both the good guys and bad guys were using language that I would never put in print. A woman was screaming words that, even as a teenager, I never used. Profanity has been commonplace in the movies for years, but I had no idea that TV had gotten so salty.

I've always been concerned about how much movies and television impact our daily lives, and so, the next morning—in the interest of research, what else?—I looked up the f-word in an old 1989 *Webster's Unabridged Dictionary* that I still have around. The word wasn't there. I did the same with the 1997 version of Webster's that I currently use. Not only did I find the f-word, but there are *thirteen* definitions. Can you think of thirteen ways to use that word? (PLEASE do not mail in your ideas.)

I looked further—again as research. There isn't a vulgar word I know that's *not* in the latest Webster's dictionary, and this has all happened in the last *eight years*. Apparently, I'm not even up to snuff on the latest cursing, because the 1997 Webster's dictionary has fifty thousand more words than the 1989 version.

Dictionaries add words after they reach a certain level of common usage, and apparently the common usage of profanity has increased greatly since 1989. I personally don't swear any more than I did eight years ago, but nowadays I hear lots of people—men and women—tossing off obscenities like they were "how are you's." I imagine these folks watch TV and take in movies regularly, so I maintain that the entertainment industry is responsible for altering the English language.

But it goes further than language. Steve McQueen played a detective in the 1968 movie *Bullitt*, which featured a classic car chase through the streets of San Francisco. Ever since, the movie industry has destroyed zillions of cars in action movies trying to duplicate—without success, I might add—the suspense in the *Bullitt* chase scene. Though these movie car chases are abysmally stupid, they've had an impact on our lives. For example, the favorite outdoor sport in Los Angeles has now become the freeway chase. The California Highway Patrol will attempt to stop some yahoo for a traffic violation, but the wrongdoer, seeing his big opportunity to become a modern-day Steve McQueen, merely puts the pedal to the metal. With all the local TV stations providing commercial-free live coverage, the cops will chase him for hours through the vast network of California freeways, frequently ranging over half the state.

Fortunately, there's not much danger of this practice catching on in Upper Michigan. They'd never be able to reach high speeds through all the potholes and road construction.

And all those explosions in the movies concern me. They blow up cars, planes, helicopters, office buildings, nuclear submarines, cities, and planets. It's scary to think that there are high-schoolers out there who consider this loads of good, clean fun and might begin to pay closer attention in chemistry class.

So why are the movie and television industries using profanity, car chases, and high explosives instead of quality dialogue and plots? Good writers are harder to find than demolition experts. Swearing consultants they can pick up anywhere.

And like the tobacco industry, they're targeting teenagers. Why spend money on sophisticated plots for a thirteen-year-old? Personally, I think they're selling the kids short.

Back in the '60's and '70's I watched a lot of TV because the programs were good. Every September I looked forward to the new "Mission Impossible" shows. Mr. Phelps never swore when he heard his assignment on the self-destruct tape. His strategies were much too sophisticated to require anything as gross as explosions, car chases, or murder. The raciest thing I ever saw on early television was "Laugh In's" Goldie Hawn skirting the edge of censorship in a bikini and body paint as she boogied between jokes.

These days I rarely go to the movies, and my television watching is pretty much limited to local news, sporting events, and the History Channel. My favorite is the stuff on World War II. It's much less violent than the current movies, and Roosevelt, Churchill, and Hitler never swore while on camera.

NECESSITY ISN'T THE MOTHER OF THESE INVENTIONS

There was a time when technology advanced out of necessity. People needed a faster way to get from Point A to Point B, and the automobile was invented. We needed a better way to make clothes, and the sewing machine came along. We wanted to stay up later, and Thomas Edison gave us the electric light. But recent technology, like Frankenstein's monster, has turned on us and dictated the pattern of our daily lives.

The reason is the invention of the microchip. Microchips are tiny, dandruff-size gizmos that are the major components of computers. Microchips have made computers very small and very brainy. Anything you buy nowadays has at least one microchip-infested computer in it. Wal-Mart will sell you a toaster that's smarter than you are. Your car will tell you to buckle your seat belt and when to pull into a service station to fill up with gas. Your filmless camera will store your wife's picture in its memory so you can transfer the image over to your PC and smooth out her wrinkles.

This technology has also polarized the human race. We have the techno-geeks who *love* all of this new stuff. Techno-geeks need very fast, high-IQ PC's for receiving e-mail from Lapland and for surfing the Internet to shop for underwear. They have runty little cellular phones in their shirt pockets, and their briefcases contain portable copying machines.

On the other end of the scale, there's the technically challenged folks—usually older—who have fallen way behind in the computer revolution. They still write letters in longhand, read books made out of actual paper, and haven't figured out why their VCR's keep blinking "12:00." They own computers but don't know it. They throw user's manuals away because of alien words like "program," "function," and "troubleshooting." I'm a middle-of-the-roader. As a writer, I use a vintage 486 PC for word processing, but my eyes glaze over if I'm forced to read the user's manual.

Computers are now running everything, but this doesn't necessarily make life easier. Last week at the supermarket checkout, the cashier didn't know the price of my apples. She began thumbing through the pages of a large fruit and vegetable code book.

"They're a dollar thirty-nine a pound," I volunteered.

"I still have to look up the code," she replied.

"Can't you just punch in a dollar thirty-nine?"

"No. The computer in the register won't accept that. We give it a code, and it tells *US* the price."

I nodded my head, sighed, and waited.

In late October it took me two hours to get off of Daylight Savings Time because I had to reset twelve digital clocks. I have to refer to the user's manuals for the harder ones, like the VCR, the dashboard clock on my Olds, and my wristwatch. It would be a lot easier if they just sold clocks with built-in receivers and twice a year beamed down the new time from one of those computer-driven communication satellites.

Recently in Ann Arbor I made a long-distance credit-card call from my motel room. By the time I'd gotten hold of the AT&T computer—it has a female voice to make us older folks feel like we're dealing with a real telephone operator—and followed its instructions, I had punched in 34 digits to get the phone on the other end to ring. By then I had forgotten why I was making the call.

In my apartment I have four remote controls, all different, and each with over forty buttons, most of which I never use. One day I tried to turn on my RCA TV set with the remote. The audio was working because I could hear Dvorak's *New World* Symphony, but the picture wasn't coming on. I discovered that I was punching the power button on my Sony CD player remote.

And so it goes. Telephones will now tell you who's calling before you even pick up the receiver. You can buy a TV set that lets you watch two channels simultaneously. Soon your new car will draw you a map and nag you if you get lost. Technology is moving at warp speed, and no one knows where it'll end. Every once in awhile I put away my pocket calculator and add and multiply with pencil and paper to see if I can still do it.

If you're a pre-baby-boomer like me, this situation may bother you, but relax. They teach computer programming in nursery school nowadays, so get your kids, grandkids, or any random young person to set your clocks, explain your telephone answering machine, or program your VCR. You may have to increase their allowance though.

RENEWING LAST YEAR'S RESOLUTIONS

This time of year everyone thinks about New Year's resolutions. I myself frequently employ the New-Month's-Resolution technique to avoid sinking to excessive depths of ignorant and disgusting behavior by year's end. But every December I still have a formidable list of character flaws to be remedied. Here's a first cut of my resolutions for this coming year. A note to my friends and family: please don't send in additions to my list.

- I resolve to wear a necktie at least four times a year so as not to forget how to tie the knot.

- Next summer, whenever my ball goes in the rough, I resolve not to sneak in winter rules by distracting my golfing partner, Jeff Jacobs, with shouts like, "Look at the moose standing on the green!"

- I resolve to learn how to put a fitted sheet on a mattress without tearing off three fingernails.

- I resolve to learn and memorize the names of the one hundred and eighty-four grandchildren of all of my cousins.

- I resolve to learn how to cook something besides rice-and-canned-soup casseroles and microwaved potatoes.

- I resolve not to use obscene gestures this winter when a passing truck splashes slush on my freshly washed car.

- I resolve to find out what rack-and-pinion steering is.

- While jogging in the Superior Dome, I resolve not to try keeping up with runners young enough to be my grandchildren in order to prove that I haven't lost it.

- When visiting my Aunt Elma in Republic, I resolve to eat only one of her prize-winning, eight-thousand-calorie prune tarts and to resist taking "one for the road."

- I resolve to improve my horseshoe throwing to lessen the risk to bystanders at our summer family outings.

- While grocery shopping, I resolve not to snarl at people who write checks in the Cash-Only line.

- I resolve not to rationalize that if one glass of wine during dinner improves my cholesterol, then two glasses will make me twice as healthy.

- I resolve to buy better quality socks so I won't have to throw away twenty pairs with holes.

- I resolve to make one more snow angel before I die.

- I resolve not to accept or give "gimme" putts longer than six feet.

- I resolve to see my first Cubs game at Wrigley Field this summer before they become pennant contenders and break their fifty-two-year-old underdog record.

- I resolve to take up snowmobiling this winter to discover the fascination.

- I resolve to get e-mail this year to shut up the people who keep telling me I can't get along without it.

- I resolve to find out where the spare tire is in my car.

GOT'CHA CHRISTMAS PRESENTS

I've always wondered about those gifts that the three wise men brought to Bethlehem. The gold I can understand, but frankincense and myrrh? Were those last-minute purchases that the wise men—pressed for ideas—picked up at Wal-Mart in Bethlehem? Or maybe they thought that Mary and Joseph needed something to kill the stable smell. However it happened, those men set a trend for eccentric and nonessential Christmas gifts that has weathered the test of time.

I've just returned from spending Christmas with out-of-town relatives, and some of the gifts opened on Christmas Eve were real lulus. All names have been withheld to protect the gift-givers and recipients and also myself (it's embarrassing to be sued by one's relatives).

I received a gift book entitled *The Outhouse Revisited*, a handsome volume with page after page of spectacular color photographs of privies. There are snow-covered outhouses in the mountains, outhouses with coat racks made from deer antlers, and an outhouse with a basketball hoop on the outside wall to amuse oneself during prolonged waits. It even has a detailed blueprint of a "three holer" with varying diameter holes for different members of the family. I will—ahem—treasure this gift for years to come.

One gift was a two-foot-high Christmas tree that belts out Christmas carols and greetings when anyone gets within range. The family dogs didn't think a great deal of the tree which kept them at bay with a hearty "Ho-ho-ho, Merrrrry Christmas."

Speaking of dogs, another gift was a video tape—William Wegman's *Mother Goose*. This tape, thanks to computer-enhanced doggy lips and audio-track dubbing, features nursery rhymes recited by real dogs. Weimaraners had most of the starring roles since they can keep a straight face better than most breeds.

There was a book called *Shoes in the Freezer, Beer in the Flower Bed*— helpful household hints discovered by two sisters who got their start writing books on the healing powers of chicken soup and then branched out. One premium hint reflected in the title is as follows: it seems that garden slugs love beer. If you pour beer in mason jars and bury them up to the lip around the perimeter of your garden, thirsty invading slugs will dive into the jars and drown in the beer. However, a downside could be that before the slugs depart for the Big Garden In The Sky, you may have to put up with their raucous slug beer-drinking songs all night long.

Someone got an automobile air purifier which cleans the air in your car when you plug it into the cigarette-lighter socket. It can be a damned nuisance, though, if you have to keep switching it with the cigarette lighter to stoke up your cigar.

If the dogs got too upset by the singing Christmas tree, here's just the thing to calm them down—*Bedtime Stories for Dogs*. Since dogs like to hear stories about other dogs and not humans, the book has fairy tales with pooches as the main characters. A few of the snappy story titles are "Goldilocks (a cocker spaniel) and the Three Cats," "The Three Little Pugs," and "Snow White and the Seven Chihuahuas."

Another Christmas present for escalating the garden-pest war: a toad house. A toad house is an igloo-shaped clay dome with a little toad door that, when placed in a damp spot in your garden, is guaranteed to attract toads. Why attract toads, you ask? To eat garden pests, of course. No instructions were included, so I haven't a clue as to how to evict unruly drunken toads should they happen to discover your beer-filled mason jars.

Here's a dandy present—a pair of lawn aerator sandals. These babies have wicked two-inch spikes on their bottoms, and you strap them to your shoes before taking a leisurely stroll around the yard. The spikes punch deep holes in the grass, thereby ventilating the sod. However, if you've already had success with your toad house, be careful where you step.

Even I contributed to the tonnage of weird gifts, giving a statue of Santa Claus—full pack on his back—riding a moose on his annual Christmas Eve journey. This was an Alaskan import. Alaskans think very highly of moose, and no doubt feel that they're far superior to reindeer in all respects, including Christmas-present delivery.

One saving grace is that you can always hustle down to the store and exchange this stuff the day after Christmas. I wonder if Joseph trotted down to the local bazaar to trade in the frankincense and myrrh for something more useful, like donkey fodder.

THE SEASONING OF A SNOWMOBILER

When I left Upper Michigan in 1951, I'd never seen a snowmobile. I'd never even *heard* of snowmobiles. A few early models were probably around, but not in Republic where I lived.

During visits in the late 70's I began to see them buzzing along the shoulders of the highways. I didn't have the faintest desire to try it; the thought of driving an open, motorized vehicle through the snow during a U.P. winter had about as much appeal as a root canal. Also, keep in mind I was living in Los Angeles where there is no such thing as pleasure-driving. You keep your eyes riveted to the roadway, trying not to incur the wrath of any Crips or Bloods in adjoining vehicles who generally keep Uzis underneath their car seats.

Why am I telling you all of this? Because my current novel-in-work has U.P. bank robbers making their getaway on snowmobiles. It's a good story, but there's just one little problem. I'd never been on a snowmobile.

Research was required. I bought several snowmobile magazines and diligently began memorizing brand names—Ski-Doo, Arctic Cat, Polaris, Yamaha—and the neat high-tech jargon—cornice jumping, trail studs, and triple-piped three bangers.

But it wasn't enough. How could I describe snowmobiling if I'd never been on one? I was like a virgin trying to write a book about sex. I had to do the deed.

I really wasn't looking forward to taking a ride on a snowmobile, but it was research and research isn't always pleasant. I contacted Myron Hillock, a snowmobile salesman at the local Honda dealer who's a seasoned racer. I told him what I needed to do, and he agreed to take me for a spin.

I knew the ride was going to be cold. Fortunately, I have a collection of state-of-the-art winter clothing from trips I've taken to the Canadian High Arctic. I put on heavy-duty storm pants over my Patagonia capilene long underwear, a wool shirt, a heavy shell and jacket, and thick woolen socks inside my big Sorel boots. It was 23 degrees outside. By the time I waddled out to the car I was breaking out in a sweat.

Myron took me to the Sled Shop on US-41 where they rent snowmobiles of all types.

"This man's never been on a snowmobile in his entire life," Myron explained to John Pritchett, the Sled Shop's owner.

Recalling the traumatic childhood experience of my first pony ride, I said to John, "Give me a gentle one."

Pritchett lent me a helmet and enthusiastically ratcheted up the chin strap tight enough to drive my beard whiskers into my skull. We decided to rent only one machine—a shiny, year-old Ski-Doo with a long seat that would easily accommodate both of us. Myron jumped on and started it up, and I tentatively got on behind. We roared across US-41 onto the network of groomed snowmobile trails.

The first thing I discovered about snowmobiling is that if you're not sealed up like hot coffee in a thermos bottle, Mother Nature will punish you. The ski mask underneath my helmet was a trifle short, and a tenth of a square millimeter of my neck was exposed. The wind immediately whistled in, depositing a thick layer of frost on my rib cage. I freed one hand and fixed the problem.

We proceeded along a groomed trail south of the highway. The scenery was stunning—pristine snow clinging to all the evergreens, no billboards, no telephone poles, no houses—a winter wonderland that you never see from the road. It's clear why the trade magazines consistently rate Upper Michigan as one of the top snowmobiling areas in the country.

"Can I take over for awhile?" I yelled into Myron's ear.

Daredevil that he is, Myron stopped and switched places with me. "First things first," I said. "Where's the brakes?"

He gave me all the basic instructions, and I grabbed the cozy, electrically heated handlebars and opened the throttle. We took off.

Someone should have told me it was so easy. Expertly steering around the curves, I gunned the throttle a bit more and assumed the role of the protagonist in my book—astride a powerful snowmobile as I sped away from the bank with a satchel of cash, whipping through the forest, the trees whizzing by like fence pickets. In reality, a snowshoer could have overtaken me at the speed I was going.

It was over all too soon. I didn't hit a single tree, and Myron never once had to leap off to save himself. An unqualified success.

Now that I'm a seasoned snowmobiler—or sledder as we veterans call ourselves—I can confidently proceed with my book. I'll be happy to field any and all questions from you readers on the subject of snowmobiling. Of course, the answers may differ somewhat from other experienced sledders.

❂ ❂ ❂

DEEP YOOPER

No doubt many of you wonder why the press keeps hammering away at President Clinton's sex life; after all, it hasn't been real news for years. It's just that they have nothing else that's juicy and bad enough to write about. Crime statistics are way down, the economy is in terrific shape with record-setting low inflation, and we've been pals with the Russians for years.

A reporter's life can be very tough when the country's in good shape. The media need something really rotten to sink their teeth into. That's what they get paid for.

But we in Marquette County, in our own small way, can help the media through this bad-news vacuum by publicizing our current airport debate. Imagine the following telephone conversation:

"Hello?"

"Is this Scoop Flanigan, star reporter for the *Detroit Free Press*?"
Scoop: "Yes, it is. Can you speak up? I can barely hear you."

"I have to keep my voice down. I want to give you a news story, and it would be very bad if I'm overheard."
Scoop: "For openers, what's your name?"

"I'm sorry, I can't give you that. Just call me Deep Yooper."
Scoop: "Deep Yooper? Like Watergate's Deep Throat?"

Deep Yooper: "You might say that."

Scoop: "What's a Yooper?"

Deep Yooper: "Never mind, just listen to what I have to say. They're going to move our airport."

Scoop: "That doesn't sound like a very newsworthy story to me. Who's going to move your airport?"

Deep Yooper: "We're not sure."

Scoop: "You have a funny accent. Are you calling from the United States?"

Deep Yooper: "Marquette, in the Upper Peninsula."

Scoop: "So someone's going to move the Marquette airport. Why?"

Deep Yooper: "We don't know."

Scoop: "You're not giving me much information here. Where are they going to move the airport?"

Deep Yooper: "To an abandoned B-52 air base."

Scoop: "Well, there's your reason. They probably want to use the long runways for larger airliners, like 747's."

Deep Yooper: "Have you ever been to Marquette?"

Scoop: "No, I haven't."

Deep Yooper: "The entire population would fit into a 747."

Scoop: "Well, I imagine that the old air base is in a convenient location for everybody."

Deep Yooper: "It's miles from nowhere, in the middle of the woods."

Scoop: "The Air Force obviously needed a highly sophisticated air terminal for servicing those nuclear bombers. Maybe they gave you folks a real good deal on the terminal."

Deep Yooper: "There is no terminal. They're going to build a brand-new one."

Scoop: "That DOES sound suspicious. Tell me, is the federal government financing this?"

Deep Yooper: "Some of it, but there's a three-million dollar shortfall."

Scoop: "Who's going to pay the rest?"

Deep Yooper: "We don't know."

Scoop: "So what are you people going to do?"

Deep Yooper: "Some of us are going to stage a protest by dressing up like Indians and throwing cases of coffee into the Marquette harbor— just as soon as the ice melts."

Scoop: "Just like the Boston Tea Party, huh? But why coffee?"

Deep Yooper: "Not too many people drink tea up here."

Scoop, getting excited: "This sounds like a good story. I'll fly up and check it out. You DO have an operational airport there right now, don't you?"

Deep Yooper: "Yes. A modern one in a convenient location. I have to hang up now. I've already been on the phone too long."

Scoop: "One more question. Do you think that one of Clinton's girlfriends may be responsible for all this?"

Deep Yooper: "It's very possible."

WHEN EVERY KID WAS A JUMPER

Back when I was a kid in Ishpeming, the Suicide Hill ski-jumping tournament was the absolute highlight of the winter season. Early on the first morning of the tournament my father and I would walk to the hill together. We took in the first practice jumps and stayed until the final entry came down the hill.

My favorite place to stand and watch was from just below the takeoff—I still call it the bump. It was so steep I always thought I was going to fall off the hill, but you could see and hear everything. In those days, they didn't have sleek, tight-fitting clothing designed to reduce aerodynamic drag. When a skier came flying off the bump, his pants and jacket crackled in the wind like exploding firecrackers. It was sheer excitement.

I loved going to Suicide because I was a ski jumper myself. In fact, *every* boy in Ishpeming was a jumper—peer pressure left you no choice. If a kid didn't ski jump, he was immediately labelled as a wimpy, chicken-livered cream puff who crept home after school to do girl things like cutting out paper dolls in the privacy of his bedroom.

My ski-jumping career began at age six when I inherited an old pair of skis from my father. They were solid maple with leather toe straps, much too long for me. The old man took them out to the woodshed and sawed a foot off the back end, leaving the toe straps near the rear edge of the ski. I didn't care; I was happy to have them.

Every neighborhood in Ishpeming had a ski jump—some big, some small. The kids built them—no adult supervision was extended nor requested. We lived at the south end of Second Street next to the LS&I ore-train tracks, so my pal Jeff Jacobs and I built a two-meter hill going down the railroad-track embankment.

It didn't take very long to discover that my hand-me-down skis needed binders if I was to continue ski jumping. With only toe straps, the skis kept flying off my feet every time I went over the bump, not a good thing to have happen when you're a ski jumper.

My father solved the problem by cutting two thick bands of rubber from an old inner tube. The rubber binders stretched from underneath the foot at the toe strap to around the heels of my galoshes. It was a big improvement, but in midair the skis still wiggle-waggled badly, often crossing as I landed, causing me to slide the rest of the way on my face. It was some time before I realized that snow jammed down the inside of my long underwear wasn't an integral part of ski jumping.

Last Saturday I went to the 111th Tournament at Suicide Hill, hoping to recapture that old excitement I knew as a kid.

The first bit of excitement was getting to the parking lot. The entrance road from M-28 has potholes the size of my Oldsmobile. Arriving European skiers must think they're competing in a U.P. version of a Nordic combined event—off-road racing and ski jumping.

The parking lot was a sea of mud. I was told that the Department of Natural Resources (DNR) won't allow it to be paved. "The area's a protected wetland," they've declared. They got the wetland part right. Cars were sinking in up to the axles.

But the hill was in good shape, and there was a large crowd on hand. I ran into several people I knew but left them standing down on the outrun. I knew where I had to be—up at the bump to see the action at close range.

I swear, they must have steepened the landing since I was a kid. I got to the ninety meter mark—about halfway up to the bump—when my lungs cried out, "Where in the #@*!! are we going?" I was catching my breath as the tournament began.

It was every bit as great as I anticipated. There's no more beautiful sight than a ski jumper in flight, leaning way out, arms at his sides, head inches from the ski tips, his body catching the air like a wing. He holds this position steady until the last split second when he bends his knees for a telemark landing. This is definitely not a sport for the faint of heart.

Did you know that *women* are jumping on Suicide now? Jeff Jacobs and I would *never* have let a girl ride our two-meter hill over on Second Street. Women have taken up hockey, boxing, cigar-smoking, and now ski jumping. Where will it all end?

The Europeans seemed to have a distinct edge over the Americans—unfortunate, but not surprising; ski jumping is far more popular in Europe. Americans like weekend sports, and ski jumping definitely doesn't fall into that category. You have to start young on small hills, work at it constantly, and gradually move up to the larger hills. Snowboarding and free-style aerobatics are the current fads in this country. This type of hot-dog skiing is actually not hard at all. Jeff and I used to execute those same death-defying spins, twists, and somersaults over on our Second Street ski jump. Of course, we never planned them in advance.

Neighborhood ski jumps in Ishpeming are a thing of the past. There'd probably be a city ordinance against them now anyway. Young local jumpers have to go to the SUNTRAC hills at Suicide Bowl—fine hills, of course, but they'd be easier to get to if someone repaired that road. Also, the DNR ought to rethink that protected wetlands business and allow the Ishpeming Ski Club to have the parking lot paved. After all, U.P. mosquitoes aren't an endangered species, yet.

BACK THEN WE ALL CARRIED KNIVES

The other day I read in the *Mining Journal* where an Ishpeming sixth-grader was expelled for having a hunting knife in his school locker. It brought home just how much times have changed. When I was going to Ishpeming Central School I *always* took a knife to school—a pocketknife. Every boy had one. In fact, during recess we played a game called Knives—some people called it Mumblypeg. No one thought a thing about it, and it never occurred to us to use the pocketknife as a weapon.

But the school had other rules, and when you broke them you suffered the consequences. Expulsion was rare. Teachers—using vigilante justice—straightened the kids out right at the scene of the crime. They used disciplinary methods that, if employed today, would have ten thousand lawyers knocking down the schoolhouse door.

In my first-grade penmanship class we were subjected to the Palmer Method. This medieval torture was designed to mold your penmanship skills, ultimately enabling you to produce finer-looking script than Thomas Jefferson used on The Declaration of Independence. One of the Palmer exercises was the dreaded oval—drawing a continuous "O," over and over as you inched across the page, forming what resembled a long roll of barbed wire. Of course, this had to done in ink, using a metal-nibbed wooden pen that required frequent dipping into the desk's built-in inkwell. The pen would maliciously piddle ink on your ovals just before you reached the end of the page.

I thought the Palmer ovals were the stupidest thing imaginable, and one day during penmanship class I rebelled. Instead of doing my ovals, I began drawing a most unflattering picture of Miss Bennalick, the first-grade teacher. She was patrolling the aisles and spotted this. Without so much as an "excuse me," she whacked my right hand solidly with her trusty wooden ruler, sending the pen flying.

"Pick up your pen and do your ovals," she barked.

If you think you have good motor skills and can do anything with your hands, try making Palmer ovals with completely numb fingers.

In the third grade I became a master at shooting spitballs with a rubber band. One afternoon while Mrs. O'Neal was droning on about the intricacies of multiplication tables, I scored a direct hit on the ear of a cute girl sitting clear across the room. I was congratulating myself on my superb markmanship when Mrs. O'Neal stormed over, grabbed a handful of my hair, and hoisted me clean out of the seat. I was marched on tiptoes over to a closet where the stationery supplies were stored. She threw me in and locked the door. It was as dark as the inside of a wolf's mouth in there with no place to sit, so I hunkered down on the floor to serve out my sentence. Time passed. Recess came and went. I became hungry and longed for my afternoon peanut butter and jelly sandwich. A kid I knew had also gotten the closet treatment from Mrs. O'Neal, and he'd claimed that starvation could be averted with the library paste stored in the closet. I groped around and found the large jar of paste. It wasn't bad, but I would've preferred peanut butter and jelly.

The pinnacle of my running afoul of scholastic law occurred in my junior year at Republic High School. One spring day in 1950 a gang of us decided to take the afternoon off from school and play baseball on the diamond south of town. After the game I ferried a load of players back to town in my newly acquired Model A Ford. We were at the top of Park City Hill (long since flattened by the Republic Mine) when who should be speeding in the opposite direction, heading for the ball diamond, but Chet Brown, the high-school principal. When Republic kids played hooky, Chet didn't bother contacting parents—he went looking for the kids himself. Chet slammed on the brakes of his '47 Pontiac, turned around, and began to chase us.

"We're dead," I cried. "He knows my car."

"Yeah, but he doesn't know who's in it," said the kid squeezed in next to me. He jammed down the hand throttle on the Model A's steering column and hung on to it with both hands. The Model A took off screaming down Park City Hill. There was nothing I could do but steer.

At the time I remember thinking, what's worse—death by car crash or having Chet Brown catch us? Chet was a fine teacher, but he had a fierce disposition when riled and would think nothing of asking a rebellious kid to step outside the classroom where they could "discuss" his behavior privately. I elected to make a run for it.

We shot through town and out the river road where we skidded to a stop at the edge of a cedar swamp, Chet not far behind. Six of us tore off into the swamp and crouched down in icy, knee-deep water while Chet searched my car looking for clues. The next morning in front of the eight o'clock assembly he unerringly named each and every hooky player. We got off with a light sentence by Chet Brown's standards—a month of staying after school to remodel the wood shop.

Those teachers are all gone now. Chet Brown passed away in his sleep last month at age ninety, and I had the honor of delivering a eulogy at his funeral. U.P. schools have other methods of dealing with delinquent behavior now. It's a far more "sophisticated" world today. Still, I can't help but wonder what would happen if we could bring back Miss Bennalick, Mrs. O'Neal, and Chet Brown and plunk them into some of those big-city classrooms where violence and drugs are all too commonplace. It would be one hell of a battle, but I know who'd win.

GIANT ASTROID CAN'T STOP PROGRESS

By now you've all heard about the astroid speeding toward earth. The following telephone conversation reports the latest development.

"Hello?"

"Is this the Marquette County Commission Chairman?"

"Yes, it is."

"My name is Hector Henshaw, President of the International Astronomical Union. Sir, I've just gotten off the phone with the President of the United States and secondly, the Governor of Michigan, who recommended that I talk to you. I'm afraid I've got some very distressing news."

<u>Commissioner:</u> "Oh? What's that?"

<u>Henshaw:</u> "You've heard about the astroid 1997 XF11 that's speeding toward earth?"

<u>Commissioner:</u> "Yes. It's going to miss the earth by 600,000 miles."

<u>Henshaw:</u> "That's what we first thought. But the latest orbital refinements indicate that it *will* strike the earth. In fact, I deeply regret to inform you that the impact point will be south of the city of Marquette at an abandoned B-52 air base. I understand that there are plans to develop a new airport there."

Commissioner: "That's right."

Henshaw: "Sir, in light of this calamitous development, be advised that you must reconsider this move."

Commissioner: "Is this some kind of joke? Are you working for the Negaunee township?"

Henshaw: "No sir, this is not a joke—you must heed my warning. The collision will be a catastrophe of unprecedented magnitude. The astroid is a mile in diameter. It will make an incredibly large crater at the point of impact."

Commissioner: "That should pose no problem. We've had a great deal of experience filling up large potholes. Have you seen our highways after the spring thaw?"

Henshaw: "It's much more serious than that. Human casualties could run extremely high if everyone isn't evacuated from the area."

Commissioner: "Also no problem. The airport site isn't anywhere near our population centers."

Henshaw: "Sir, you don't understand. The site can't be used for a commercial airport. In order to predict the consequences, the federal government must acquire the land to accommodate the astrophysicists, geologists, and other world scientists who'll be studying the impact site over the next thirty years."

Commissioner: "The astroid won't hit for thirty years? Then there's no reason we can't operate the airport until then."

Henshaw: "I'm sorry, that's just not possible. This study will require a sizeable installation. The government will need to erect a number of buildings at the impact site."

Commissioner: "Hmmm. (thinking) Buildings you say? We already *have* quite a few buildings there; unoccupied, as a matter of fact. There's no reason why we couldn't give the government a good deal on them."

Henshaw: "I don't think so. The government will want to design the buildings to its own specifications."

Commissioner: "What would you say to a thirty-year lease on as many large commercial buildings as you'll need for only ten percent of what it would cost the government to build them?"

Henshaw: "Ten percent? Hmmm. (thinking)"

Commissioner: "We already have excellent support facilities there. A hotel, a large health club, and even a golf course where your scientists can relax after a hard day of predicting casualties.

(Now, with more enthusiasm) "And if they're going to be flying in—day and night—from all over the world, the runway is even long enough to make it an international airport. It's an ideal location for what you need."

Henshaw: "Your offer *does* sound attractive."

Commissioner: (even more enthusiastically) "Other businesses are sure to flock in, once the word gets around about the congregation of world scientists. We'd have restaurants, shops, and theaters. This will really put the new airport area on the map."

Henshaw: "Sir, you don't understand. It won't *be* on the map after the astroid hits."

Commissioner: (enthusiasm undampened) "Nothing is forever, but it'll be an economic boom while it lasts."

Henshaw: "Sir, I'll be attending an emergency meeting with the President and his cabinet tomorrow morning in Washington. I'll pass your proposal along. I'm certain that it will be well received."

Commissioner: "We could call it Astroid City."

Henshaw: "Astroid City. I like that."

✿ ✿ ✿

ENTERING THE PORTALS OF GEEZERHOOD

Several years ago, whenever I was shooting the bull with the guys at work and the conversation turned to retirement, I headed for the door. After all, who wanted to discuss ho-hum drivel like pensions, Social Security, or Medicare—subjects of interest only to old far . . . excuse me, senior citizens. Back then I had more urgent items on my agenda, like promotions, money, and women.

Well, guess what, folks? My birthday is coming up this week, and the big *SIX FIVE* is knocking at my door. I'm about to enter the portals of geezerhood.

All my life I've pictured sixty-five-year-olds as crusty old curmudgeons who spend their days sitting in rocking chairs on the front porch, smoking corncob pipes, and saying howdy to passing neighbors. A cane stays hooked over the back of the rocker in case they feel up to strolling downtown to the barber shop to swap lies with their crusty-old-curmudgeon cronies.

I can't possibly be sixty-five years old! I don't even *own* a rocker, a corncob pipe, or a cane. The only time I go to the barber shop is to get a trim. Although, I've noticed lately that my barber has started clipping long hairs growing out of my ears. In years past, I don't remember barbers ever doing that. They must be getting more fastidious.

My friend, Jeff Jacobs, *does* fall into the crusty-old-curmudgeon category. But he's a lot older than I am—eight months, if memory serves me right. He tells stories of how things were when he was a kid—something that old geezers like to do. I must admit, some of those stories *do* have a familiar ring. The other day he asked me if I remembered how the family doctor would come over to the house whenever we got sick.

"Of course I remember," I said. "What's so strange about that?"

"I rest my case, you old retard," Jeff chortled. "You're just as ancient as *I* am. Doctors quit making house calls fifty years ago."

That doesn't surprise me. You can't trust doctors. Back in the sixties, one told me that I should cut back on my wine consumption. I took his advice and cut it out entirely. Last year my Marquette doctor said that a glass of wine a day would improve my LDL cholesterol, whatever that is. I wish they'd make up their minds. And I really hate it when they examine me and say, "You're in pretty good shape for a person your age." What do they mean, "a person your age"? Would I be in *rotten* shape if my driver's license read *1963* instead of 1933?

I think I'm as good as ever—in fact, my memory is phenomenal. I can still remember how to put a patch on a tire inner tube. Multiplying and dividing on my slide rule is no problem. And the capitals of all forty-eight states—I can name them off right now. Yesterday, I *did* forget why I walked into the bathroom, but you have to expect some mental lapses from time to time.

There *are* a few puzzling aspects of getting older. Lately I've noticed that when I open the *Mining Journal* the first thing I turn to is the obituaries. Why is that? I used to look at the sports page first. Speaking of sports, now when I see the springtime *Sports Illustrated* Swimsuit Edition on the newsstand, I keep thinking that there was a good reason I liked that particular issue, but I forget what it was. Probably because it contains the Chicago Cubs roster for the new season.

I'll always remember when I was a kid, my old man would let out this loud grunt every time he got up off the sofa. I could never figure out why he did that. Now *I'm* doing it and I don't know why.

Becoming a senior citizen does have its advantages. Waiters and waitresses now call me *SIR* all the time. I like that. On the third of each month I receive a check from the United States Government, and they don't expect a thing in return. And the movie theatre will give me two dollars off on tickets. It would encourage me to see more movies except that I can't seem to get up out of those damned theater seats after sitting for two hours.

There was lots more I was going to say, but it's time for my nap now.

CALIFORNIA:
THE LAND OF BULLETPROOF GLASS

Since I moved back to the U.P., people are always saying to me, "You moved *here* from *California*? You must have stayed out on the beach too long without a hat!" Strange how hard it is to convince folks that California isn't exactly the land of milk and honey. I periodically reinforce this knowledge with visits to the perpetual-sunshine state. In fact, I just returned.

Riding the escalator down to the baggage claim area at the Los Angeles International Airport, I secured the button on my wallet pocket and nimbly stepped to the right to allow the stampeding Los Angelinos to rush past me down the steep moving stairs. Muscling my way into the wall of humanity at the luggage carousel, I grabbed my suitcase and struggled out to the street.

I got into the first cab in the long line waiting at the curb.

"Marina del Rey," I enunciated slowly into the small opening in the bulletproof glass shield between the driver and myself. From previous experience, it was a reasonable assumption that the cabby spoke little English.

As soon as he had deciphered my directions, the cabby growled in irritation. He had hoped for a much larger fare to downtown Los Angeles. Ramming the gas pedal to the floorboard, he expertly plunged the cab into the raging river of airport traffic.

I keep a 1971 Chevy pickup truck garaged at a friend's home in Marina del Rey, and the first order of business was getting it running after six months of inactivity. At a nearby gas station I checked the truck's fluids and filled it with gas after prepaying the non-English-speaking attendant housed in his bulletproof enclosure.

The local rules of the road came back quickly as I shot up an on-ramp of the San Diego Freeway and deftly cut off a brand-new, cream-colored BMW in the slow lane. On Los Angeles freeways you don't use turn signals for lane changes. Tipping off the other drivers of your intentions is extremely foolhardy; it allows them to take appropriate countermeasures. The old Chevy truck is also a big advantage. The BMW and Mercedes drivers assume that I'm not insured and give me plenty of room.

On Sunday morning I picked up a copy of the *Los Angeles Times*. If you're thinking about moving to Southern California, better take a peek at the real-estate prices in the classifieds. You'd like a Beverly Hills address, you say? The *average* price of Beverly Hills homes listed in the *Times* is well over a million dollars—that's *AVERAGE*—and there are some pretty tacky locations in south Beverly Hills. Housing prices in my old stomping grounds in Marina del Rey go from $750,000 on up. Of course you could always rent while saving up your first million, but that may present a problem, too. They want $1500 or more a month for a one-bedroom unfurnished apartment in the better parts of Los Angeles County.

I went on to read the Metro section. It seems that the mail carriers in nearby El Camino Village—sounds like a nice peaceful little hamlet, doesn't it?—are being escorted by sheriff's deputies to prevent assaults and mail thefts by organized gangs. This is not an isolated incident; handling mail in Los Angeles has become a dangerous occupation. In fact, many of the post offices there now have bulletproof glass installed at the service counters, although I'm not clear if it's to protect the postal employees from the customers or vice versa.

And of course, there were the usual newspaper reports of multiple homicides and assorted torture and strangulation cases, but no one pays much attention to those anymore.

There was *one* piece of good news in the paper, however. Los Angeles no longer has the worst drivers in the nation. They've fallen to fourth, behind New York, Boston, and Washington, D.C. That made me feel a whole lot safer.

But if *kinky* is your cup of tea, then you'd definitely love California. One TV channel featured a provocative little item called "Spanking the Spice Girls." Don't ask me for details; I missed it. Monday night's Special Assignment on another channel was a report on "Backyard Pornography." I have to admit, that's one problem with living in the U.P. It's too cold up here most of the year to participate in some of these really neat outdoor activities that Californians are so good at.

So there you are. If you're an independently wealthy, bilingual, experienced stock-car-race driver with bizarre sexual inclinations, and only trust air that you can see, then Southern California may be the place for you. Personally, I'll stay in the U.P.

HOLY COW! COULD THIS BE THE YEAR OF THE CUBS?

I'm hurriedly dashing off this piece since the subject matter may be as short-lived as a snowflake on a hot stove.

Today is the ninth of June, 1998—mark the date on your calendar. The Chicago Cubs are in first place.

"Holy Cow!" as the late Cubs announcer Harry Carey was fond of saying. The earthshaking significance of this is obvious to baseball fans, but for those of you who think that a pop-up is a toaster waffle, I'll explain.

The Chicago Cubs are the enduring underdogs of baseball. Over the past ninety years they've always found ways to elude a championship season. The last time they were in a World Series was in 1945—they lost to the Detroit Tigers. And if you're talking about *winning* a World Series, you have to go all the way back to 1908.

It's interesting; other teams, after compiling a humongous, long-term losing record, have packed up and left their respective towns. Just sound economics. But not so the Cubs. Every season finds a staunch army of Chicago fans packing into Wrigley Field, producing sellouts for many of the home games. Until only recently all of these games were played during the day, and most of them still are.

Who are these people sitting out in the bleachers season after season, courting skin cancer with their shirts off, clutching hot dogs and cups of beer while squinting into the sun toward home plate? One thing's for sure, they're not aerospace CEO's or techno-geniuses from the Silicon Valley. You won't find Bill Gates at a Cubs game. No, these folks are the hard-hat, lunch-bucket types—obviously on night shift—who come out to cheer for a team that—like themselves—has a lot of experience and appreciation for the unexpected potholes in the road of life.

And they're *loyal*. If the opposing team hits a ball into the stands at Wrigley Field for a home run, the fans immediately throw it back onto the field. After all, who wants to keep a tainted souvenir baseball hit by some wimpy Atlanta Brave?

I think many Cub fans are ex-right-fielders. Right fielders know what it's like to be perched on the fringes of baseball. When I was a kid, anytime we could lay our hands on a bat, a ball, and a few gloves, we'd choose up sides. Because of my third-rate motor skills I was always the last to be picked, and the humiliation became complete when I was assigned to play right field. Very few balls were hit to right field, so there was little chance I could screw up the defense.

Needless to say, I'm a dyed-in-the-wool Cubs fan and have been since the 1940's. I picked it up from my father who was a veteran rooter for underdog baseball teams: the St. Louis Browns, the Washington Senators, and, of course, the Chicago Cubs. The old man absolutely hated the New York Yankees who, over the decades, have been one of the best teams in baseball. He didn't want to hear about the feats of Mickey Mantle, Roger Maris, or Whitey Ford.

"Why don't you like the good teams?" I asked him early on.

"Any damn fool can root for the New York Yankees," the old man growled. "But it takes real guts to root for the Chicago Cubs."

Over the years the Cubs became my standard of non-excellence. Whenever I've had trouble achieving a goal, I cheer up by saying to myself, "Ah, but you're not doing as badly as the Cubs."

But now they've won ten straight games. The last time the Cubs did that was in the early seventies. What does this mean—is it a trend? Nobody knows. What if they go all the way to the World Series and win? Don't even think about it. It would be like a flying saucer landing on the White House lawn—too awesome to contemplate. The fans could burn Chicago down out of sheer enthusiasm.

I'm not even sure that I really *want* the Cubs to become successful. Like my old man, I'm hooked on the underdogs. For years my favorite team in the American League was the Cleveland Indians. The last time they'd gone to the World Series was back in 1954 where they lost four straight to the New York Giants. Year after year they couldn't do anything right, yet I cheered them on.

Then a strange thing happened. The Indians got good. They've gone to the World Series two out of the last three years, and they're well-entrenched in first place right now. I don't root for them anymore, they're not my kind of team.

I'd better calm down. It's only early June, and anything can and probably will happen to the Cubs. By the time this article appears in print they may have sunk to third place or worse—it's happened before. So don't judge my enthusiasm too harshly. I'm just savoring the moment.

VISITING AN OLD FRIEND

Recently I went out to the airport—as many of you did—to see the B-17 bomber that the Yankee Air Museum had flown up from Willow Run. I watched as the airplane flew in from the south, her polished aluminum skin glinting in the sunlight. When I learned that five dollars would get me a tour of the inside of the bomber, I quickly fished out my cash and stood in line with several gray-haired gentlemen who'd brought their grandchildren.

The B-17, with its two-thousand-mile range and nine tons of bombs, was used for daring daylight raids on Germany during World War II. Hitler threw everything he had at the B-17, and the bombers sustained enormous losses in the early days of the war. But this tough old bird didn't earn its nickname—The Flying Fortress—for nothing. Bristling with armament, the B-17's shot down a staggering number of German fighters who tried to intercept them, and their bombs wreaked such havoc on Germany's industrial centers that they were instrumental in winning the war.

The line moved up toward the airplane. "This is one of the later models of the Fortress," I remarked casually to some people next to me. "That gun turret beneath the nose plexiglass was a late addition." They stared at me, thinking that perhaps I'd been a crewman on one of these famous planes.

But no, I was only eight years old when the U.S. got into the war. However, the smoke hadn't cleared from Pearl Harbor when I began building model airplanes. I quickly became a veritable fountain of knowledge on every World War II military aircraft ever produced—and not just U.S. planes: British, Russian, German, and Japanese as well. If Hitler had ever sent over a squadron of ME-109 Messerschmitts to carry out a sneak-attack on Ishpeming, I would have identified them immediately.

In the 1940's, model airplanes were, more-or-less, miniatures of the real plane, inside and out. They were horrendously difficult to build. The instructions were detailed and complex, describing how the fuselage and wing ribs were to be cut out of sheets of balsa wood and then carefully connected together with balsa-wood stringers to form the aircraft structure. The airplane's outer skin was tissue paper, spot-glued to the structure and lightly sprinkled with water to tighten the paper. Then, colored airplane dope was applied to the tissue paper, making it realistic and durable. The final step was the best: putting on the insignia decals—a white star in a blue circle for a U.S. plane, an Iron Cross for Germany, or a red rising sun for Japan.

One day, pressing my nose against the window of my favorite hobby shop in Ishpeming, I saw it. A model of the B-17 Flying Fortress. Holy smoke; an honest-to-gawd, four-engine flying model of the most famous bomber of the war—with thirteen machine guns! I had to have it. I rushed into the store and was politely informed that the kit cost the outrageous sum of a dollar and a quarter.

When I approached my old man for financial assistance, he looked at me like I'd lost my mind. "A buck an' a quarter fer a model airplane? That kind of money'll buy a day's worth of groceries!"

So I scrimped and saved—foregoing my other two vices—Mounds candy bars and *Green Lantern* comic books—until I had the money. I ran down to the store and bought the B-17 kit.

If I'd thought that my Douglas Dauntless Navy dive bomber model had been tough to build, the B-17 bomber model was much worse. For weeks—running well into summer vacation—I worked on that plane. Blood flowed freely from the Exacto-knife cuts on my fingers as I excavated the dozens of ribs from sheets of balsa. My bedroom reeked of Testor's model cement as I glued the whole assembly together. I had to anchor rubber bands inside each of the four engine nacelles, allowing the propellers to spin in order to fly the plane. This step was ridiculous because after all that work no kid in his right mind would have flown that model airplane. By now it was a work of art and much too precious and fragile for the rigors of flight.

It was done. The silver-colored airplane dope I'd used gleamed softly in the light from my bedroom window. Each of the thirteen machine-gun barrels sticking out from the various turrets and ports had been painted a lethal black. The crowning touch was an array of tiny swastikas beneath the pilot's cockpit window to show how many Nazi fighters my plane had shot down.

I carefully hung the B-17 model from the ceiling, and every evening for months I lay on my back in bed, admiring it before turning out the lights. It was the most difficult task I'd ever undertaken.

The other day when my turn came at the airport, I climbed into the B-17 and walked reverently through the fuselage, underneath the top gun turret, along the narrow catwalk through the bomb bay, past the navigator's and radio operator's positions, and out the hatch by the waist gunner's stations. I had never been close to a real B-17 Flying Fortress before, but I recognized every rib and longeron. I was visiting an old friend.

❂ ❂ ❂

I HAVE MAIL!

I don't want to hear any more snide comments like, "What—you don't have e-mail?" because I've gone ahead and done it. I've got e-mail. I just took delivery on a 266MHz, 64 megabyte RAM, 4.3 gigabyte hard drive, Pentium II computer, and not only do I have e-mail, I have a whole slew of other techno-stuff that'll take me forever to figure out.

It was hard to give up the old PC. As a writer, I can only conjure up about two hundred words an hour, and my clunky old 486 was more than up to the task. When I bought it back in 1993, it was on the cutting edge of technology and cost three thousand dollars. Today, thanks to brainy, hard-working elves out in the Silicon Valley doubling computer speeds every six months, my 486 is now totally obsolete and maybe worth a hundred bucks. However, it could still do the job.

But I kept hearing phrases like, "web site," "doohickey-dot-com," and "surfing the net for pictures of naked women." This advanced technical jargon tweaked my intellectual curiosity, and I began thinking about a new computer. People I know were very supportive, tossing out comments like, "You must get online. Last night I was chatting on e-mail with this reindeer herder in Lapland . . ." I was skeptical. I don't know any reindeer herders in Lapland, and if I did, I'd probably write them a letter or call. At least on the telephone I don't have to worry about typos.

But I finally caved in and ordered a new PC. Don Szenina (I highly recommend him, incidentally) from MicroAge in Ishpeming brought it over to my apartment. He spent fifteen minutes hooking it up and then hung around for several hours educating me on how to use it. I still haven't figured out everything, but I'm learning.

This new PC came with fancy speakers and sound effects, but I have to determine how to kill some of the noises. For example, the screen saver has whirling electronic parts on a black background accompanied by annoyingly loud hi-tech squeaks, grunts, and chirps. From my bedroom it sounds as if someone's prying off my front door with a crowbar. Screen savers can be changed, but I didn't know how to do it, so I finally shut off the whole damned computer and went to bed.

The new PC has a calculator that can be brought up on the screen to assist in balancing your checkbook. I won't be using that, though. If I did, it wouldn't be long before I'd forget how to do simple arithmetic with a paper and pencil. Computers are sneaky that way.

I also have the latest copy of Microsoft Golf, and if you golfers think that electronic golf is a piece of cake, I suggest that you give it a try. On my first attempt, I was nineteen over par after six holes, and that was after taking several mulligans. To make matters worse, the computer makes snotty little comments when you make a bad shot. "That's rough stuff over there!" it taunts nastily when you slice the ball into the electronic high grass. I don't need insults from hi-tech hardware. I get enough from my friends.

But being on-line is really neat for researching all kinds of things. There's a brainy software package called a search engine that can take any subject you give it, gallop off into the bowels of the Internet, and in no time at all lug back megatons of data. I tested the search engine with several profound subjects. Do you know how much online information is currently available on diarrhea? More than you'll ever want.

E-mail is really quite amazing. My machine had been plugged in for less than two hours when I got an e-mail from a guy in California who I hadn't heard from in *five years*! How did he do that? People must belong to a secret e-mail society where the members prowl hyperspace, looking for rookies.

I'll give you my e-mail address—jharju@bresnanlink.net—but don't expect to chat with me by e-mail unless you make the first move. So far I've only figured out how to reply to messages, not initiate them.

There's scads of other software that came with my PC that I haven't even looked at yet: an encyclopedia; a map maker; a graphics package to make birthday, sympathy, and get-well cards; a Billboard music guide; and the complete list of video movies you can find at Blockbuster. And if I run out of time trying to learn how all of this stuff works, they have an electronic day planner, which would be handy if I ever figure out how to install it.

THE HIAWATHA MUSIC FESTIVAL: A TIME WARP

In the late fifties and throughout the sixties I was doing all the important things that young men at the time did. One was folk music. I regularly made the rounds of Los Angeles coffeehouses to see and hear guitar and banjo pickers like Doc Watson, Josh White, Pete Seeger, Bud and Travis, and others. I even organized my own hootenannies, inviting people over to sing, play guitar, or just listen and partake of the cheap California wine that I bought for $1.65 a gallon. I got pretty fair on the guitar and for many years gave group and private lessons, demonstrating my sexy blues brush and lightning-fast hammer-ons to beginning students.

Then, as the years went by, folk music drifted out of vogue. At the same time, for reasons which now escape me, I became involved with scaling the corporate ladder in the aerospace business. I picked up the guitar less and less. By the nineties, when I took early retirement and began to write (books, not songs), the guitar case was rarely opened.

So, a few weeks ago, when my uncle Arvid and I went to the Twentieth Annual Music Festival at Marquette Tourist Park, I didn't expect a whole lot. I'd come to the conclusion that over the years folk music had gone the way of tie-dyed trousers and long sideburns.

Arvid and I sat down to listen. He tapped his cane and I tapped my foot in time to many talented musicians—Robin and Linda Williams, the Laurel Canyon Ramblers, and others—singing and playing music I hadn't heard in a long time. U.P. home-grown, nineteen-year-old Erik Koskinen played guitar, blew harmonica, and sang blues simultaneously—a neat trick requiring a harmonica harness around the neck and lots of practice. Koskinen may become another Bob Dylan as he was in his early years.

There were other things to see. One vendor had a truckload of old-timey 33 rpm records. Do you remember when 33 rpm's were state of the art—replacing 78's? People back then were saying, "More than one song on each side of the record? What will they think of next!"

Under a tree a woman was spinning yarn from wool taken right off the sheep's back, although she admitted that she'd washed it first (the wool, not the sheep). She'd grab a handful of wool, feed it into the wheel, and form a continuous whirling strand of yarn. I asked her how much she could spin in a day, and she held up a bundle of yarn the size of a cantaloupe and said, "This took all of yesterday." It wasn't much to show for a day's work, but she didn't seem to mind.

A blacksmith was pulling brightly glowing iron rods from his forge and noisily pounding them into submission with a large hammer. He was making weathervanes. Children watching him didn't know what he was doing, but it sure looked like fun. When I was a kid, there were still enough horses left in Ishpeming to allow blacksmiths to make a decent living. That was one of the things I wanted to be when I grew up. Blacksmiths were strong, and they didn't have to wear corduroy knickers, comb their hair, or wash their hands.

The whole festival scene was a time warp back to the forties or even earlier. There were thousands of people there, music-loving, gentle folks with children who didn't have spiky haircuts or electronic music wired into their ears. No one left trash scattered around, like most people do in parks. They gathered on the wooden platforms spread around on the grass, dancing in overalls and clunky-looking shoes to anything and everything: gospel music, protest songs, blues, or ballads. One woman, dancing for hours by herself, didn't need any music at all. It seemed as though she was accompanying birds singing in the nearby trees.

When we got up to leave, I couldn't help but wonder where these people go on Sunday night. What kind of lives do they lead in this fast-paced, e-mail world? It's as though their rightful place was right there in that park, playing, singing, and dancing forever.

I went home and took my 1927 Martin guitar out of the case. It needed tuning badly, and that took me awhile because you lose the knack without practice. I could still remember "Freight Train Blues," albeit it sounded jerky, and the hammer-ons in "Darlin' Cory" killed my fingertips because I'd lost the calluses.

The festival had something called Open Mike, where anyone could get up on the stage with their guitar and try not to make a fool out of themselves. I used to be as good as some of the "open mikers" I'd heard that day. Maybe if I get back in practice, next year I'll wow the audience with "The Pig Song," "Rye Whiskey," or even "Plastic Jesus." Some of those treasured oldies deserve to be saved for posterity.

A POWERBALL JACKPOT WOULD SOLVE MY PROBLEMS

Recently a group of people won a big 292 million-dollar Powerball jackpot. It was headline news for days prior to the drawing, not because of the huge amount of money involved—after all, our government spends much more than that on hi-tech satellites to peek into Saddam Hussien's living room. What kept it in the news were all of the wacky things that folks went through just to buy the tickets.

People living in states like Michigan that don't have Powerball drove for hours to get to convenience stores across the state line where they stood in long lines for more hours, braving all kinds of weather to get their tickets. When the store owners tried to lock their doors at the close of business, fist fights broke out. Others in line didn't seem to care because they came prepared with sleeping bags, cooking utensils, and food. They camped out on the sidewalk until the place opened the following morning.

I wish someone would explain the economics of lotteries to me. Why is it that no one gets excited when the jackpot is say, ten million dollars, yet they begin foaming at the mouth when it climbs over 200 million? Is ten million dollars not worth the time and trouble? Will these people have trouble making ends meet with only ten million? Will the new roof on the deer camp have to wait another year?

It gets even more puzzling when the media interviews the new millionaire. Newsmen shove cameras and microphones into the face of the lucky stiff, asking him, "With all this money, what changes will you make in your life?"

The winner chuckles modestly and replies in all seriousness, "Oh, not much. The wife and I are gonna slap a coat of paint on the old homestead, I guess. But I work with such a swell bunch of fellas over at CESSPOOLS R'US that I figgur I'll just keep my old job, pumpin' out septic tanks."

People will buy Powerball and state lotto tickets for years, but when they finally hit the jackpot they're not inclined to change their lifestyle. The reason? Most people—whether they realize it or not—haven't given any thought on how to deal with sudden, overwhelming wealth.

I don't buy lotto tickets, but I've given a lot of thought to dealing with immense wealth. If I bought a lotto ticket and won some $292 million, you'd better *believe* there'd be changes. Powerball players may want to take some notes here.

My new home would be a modest, unpretentious structure of roughly twenty-thousand square feet with enough bedrooms to house my twenty-four-hour staff. Being an avid reader, I'd have an extensive library with an electric cherry picker so I could glide around the thirty-foot-high bookshelves. The property would have to be deep to accommodate the nine-hole golf course in the backyard—completely enclosed, of course, to allow for winter play. I wouldn't buy a snowblower because my three-hundred-yard-long driveway would have defrosters imbedded in the concrete.

My chauffeur-driven stretch limo would have a wedge-like drooping hood, giving it aerodynamic stealth characteristics to avoid police radar. Also a state-of-the-art magnetic force field would deflect the flying slush from the passing trucks on US-41 in the winter. The interior would have plenty of handy gadgets in back—a PC for my writing and solitaire games and a whole array of kitchen appliances so my chef could prepare me a snack while I watched the Packers game on the 32-inch television set. It would also be the only car in existence with a wine cellar.

I wouldn't care *where* they put the county airport, because I wouldn't use it anymore. I'd have a helipad on the roof of my house, and every time I got the urge, I'd ring up my pilot to bring the chopper around and buzz me down to Milwaukee, Chicago, or Detroit to connect with my chartered Concorde flights to London, Paris, or wherever. Or in case I wanted to take in a Cubs game, the pilot could just put the helicopter down on the roof of my condominium high above the press box at Wrigley Field in Chicago. The condo would have a hotline down to the Cubs dugout because, quite frankly, they could use some extra help when it comes to making pitching changes.

Would I keep writing these newspaper columns? Are you kidding? I'd buy the whole newspaper, take over the editorial page, and every day I'd enrich your life with my valuable opinions on a wide variety of subjects.

I have lots of other thoughts on the subject, but I have to close now. Tomorrow is senior-discount day at Econofoods, and I haven't finished clipping the grocery coupons out of last Sunday's paper.

HOME-BUYING FEVER:
A DEADLY DISEASE

A few months ago, in a moment of sheer madness, I violated one of my trusted maxims of life.

I bought a home magazine.

Home magazines are dream books telling you how to reach a state of eternal bliss simply by acquiring a home that would make Buckingham Palace look like a fixer-upper. The particular magazine that I bought featured timber-frame houses. Back at my apartment I leafed through page after page of brilliantly color photographs of cathedral-like beamed ceilings soaring high above expansive walnut-panelled living areas appointed in rough-hewn posts and beams—the ideal environment for a writer.

My breathing quickened and my temperature shot up. I began salivating. Omigawd, I thought, I knew what it was. I was experiencing the symptoms of a dread disease that had afflicted me many years earlier.

I had home-buying fever again.

My agonies with this malady began in 1964. My second wife-to-be and I were carrying on a few courtship activities (not what you think—this was 1964) on the sofa in my cozy seventy-five-dollar-a-month rented house in Santa Monica, California.

"Did you know your ceiling has a big crack in it?" she asked, looking upward over my shoulder.

"So what?" I muttered hotly into her ear.

"Don't you think we ought to fix it?"

I didn't realize at the time, but I was about to find myself on intimate terms with Martha Stewart's mother. Months later, we had replastered and painted the ceiling and steamed twenty-seven layers of wallpaper off the walls, replacing them with fancy decorator burlap. Somehow during that period we'd found time to get married.

"It's silly to keep spending money fixing up a rental," my bride declared. "We need a home of our own."

Without warning, home-buying fever struck. For weeks we were chauffeured around Los Angeles County in realtors' Cadillacs until we found a darling three-bedroom place two blocks from the ocean for the outrageously high sum of thirty-six thousand dollars.

"I love it!" my wife exclaimed enthusiastically in our new living room. "But we've got to steam off that horrible wallpaper."

Weeks later I was on the roof of our new house helping the man I'd hired to install the fifty-foot-high antenna necessary to get TV reception to the house's low-lying position at the beach.

"Your wood shingles're pretty dry," the antenna specialist observed. "You should put on some log oil to keep 'em from cracking any further."

"How much will I need?" I asked, gazing at the vast expanse of shingles on the roof.

"Oh, eight or ten gallons ought'a do it," he told me.

That roof sucked up ten gallons of log oil like it was an aperitif cocktail. I'd bought a new pickup truck to haul wallpaper, paint, and carpeting for my wife's interior renovation of the house, so I also began trucking large quantities of log oil home from the store.

"While you're at it," my wife said, "why don't you pick up some bricks to lay down in the backyard so the dogs won't dig." We had acquired two German shepherd puppies who were busily engineering an escape by tunneling under the new fence I'd built around the backyard.

And on it went. Finally, four years later, the house was in great condition. With a thousand gallons of log oil on them, the roof shingles were healthy. All of the rooms were wallpapered, painted, and carpeted to my wife's specifications. We'd just worked off the second mortgage. Everything was shipshape.

Then, one morning my wife said, "Did you hear that noise down at the beach last night? It sounded like gunfire. I tell you, this neighborhood is really going downhill. I think we ought to move."

Home-buying fever raged again until we found a delightful, two-story, contemporary on a one-acre hillside lot up in Topanga Canyon, a mere twenty-four miles from where I worked. This one cost me the staggering sum of forty-five thousand dollars. The house had a stunning view of the canyon, which was even more spectacular from the vantage point of the flimsy scaffolding that I erected to paint the exterior walls.

While I was building an enclosed dog run at the back of our lot, I got to meet my new neighbor. He stomped over shouting, "Why are you pouring concrete on my property?"

Once the property-line debate was settled, I began clearing the flammable sagebrush that grew in abundance all over the large lot. For weeks I chopped and stacked, amassing a huge pile. When the local fireman came by to give me a controlled burning permit he pointed to a tree growing next to my driveway exclaiming, "My gawd, look at that!"

"What? The tree?" I asked.

"It's not a tree," he replied. "It's poison oak. That's the biggest stand I've ever seen. It almost never gets that big, but I can see that you've got ideal growing conditions for poison oak here."

By 1972 I'd somehow become divested of houses (and wives

and dogs) and have since lived a relatively serene existence free of home-buying fever. That is, until I bought that damned timber-frame magazine.

Last week, fever raging anew, I decided to see the real thing and flew out to New England where timber-frame house builders abound. A salesman in New Hampshire showed me a nice timber-frame model home which was just about the right size. Noting that I appeared interested, he informed me that I could have the same home in Marquette, ready to move in, for about five.

"Five? What do you mean five?" I asked.

"Five hundred thousand," he replied.

"*Dollars?*" I exclaimed.

"That's right." he said. "But, of course, the land would be extra."

As I walked back toward my rental car, I could feel my temperature going down, the saliva in my mouth was drying up, and my breathing was returning to normal. I'd finally found a miraculous cure for home-buying fever.

ON DA ROAD WITH DA YOOPERS

What words come to mind when someone mentions Da Yoopers? Comical? Zany? Absurd? Rowdy? All of the above certainly apply, of course, but if you think that those goofy Yooper songs, like "Rusty Chevrolet," were dreamed up by these guys at beery binges similar to the second week of deer camp, you'd be wrong. I know, because a few weeks ago I had the privilege of hitting the road with this famous U.P. band when they did a gig at the Central Wisconsin State Fair in Marshfield. Incidentally, Da Yoopers don't go on the road in a rusty Chevrolet—they have a Ford bus with plush reclining seats.

On the bus I sat next to Da Head Yooper himself, Jimmy DeCaire— a savvy entrepreneur who built Da Yooper organization from scratch in the early 1970's. Jimmy goes to great lengths to cultivate the well-known Yooper image. Not only can he sharpen his Yooper accent at the drop of a "th," but he conducts lengthy discourses on the origin of the accent itself. He'll also tell you that he was a D student in school, but I have to seriously doubt that.

DeCaire was writing a song during the five-hour ride down to Marshfield, getting inspiration from nothing stronger than black coffee. He and Jim Belmore, the lead guitarist, generally conspire on the lyrics for Da Yooper songs. Belmore, an accomplished musician in many genres, also writes the music, creates the arrangements, and conducts band rehearsals. However, the other band members claim that Belmore's major accomplishment lies in the fact that he's eaten pizza at every meal for 31 years.

Reggy Lusardi, a tall, beefy bass player, maintains that Da Yoopers hired him expressly to sit in the back of the bus to provide traction during the winter. Guitarist Danny Collins is 43 years old and claims that he's still a virgin, although he's trying hard to change that. Veteran drummer Bobby Symons, another heavyweight, wanted to take up a career as a sumo wrestler in Negaunee but couldn't find any competition. Lynn Coffey is the only female band member, declaring that she's Da Yooper's token woman. There's nothing token about her. A graduate of NMU, Lynn is DeCaire's business partner, handling bookings and other commercial activities from Da Yooper's nerve center in the basement of the Tourist Trap. I should also mention that she's a wizard on the keyboard. An attractive, blue-eyed blonde, Lynn looks as though she should be crooning old romantic favorites like "Some Enchanted Evening." Instead, she belts out the words to "Fish Fight," another Yooper standby, with verses like,

"You smell just like a can of worms bakin' in th'sun,

There's fish guts hangin' from yer chin . . ."

As we were unloading in Marshfield (Da Yoopers also travel with two jam-packed large trucks), a good-looking young lady, spotting the large "Da Yoopers" logo on the sides of the vehicles, flashed me an admiring smile and asked, "Oh, are you playing in Marshfield this weekend?"

"We sure are," I replied, trying to look cool, like a professional musician. What the heck, I thought, I may as well contribute in the best way I can—interacting with the female fans—to allow the band to concentrate totally on their gig.

Da Yoopers have fourteen people in their road entourage, and everyone pitched in to get things ready. The band members lugged their various instruments onto the stage, along with amplifiers and miles of cord, and spent an hour or more getting set up and plugged in, followed by decibel checks with Da Yooper in-house sound engineer. My 1927 Martin guitar runs strictly on fingerpower, and I never cease to be amazed at how much electronic equipment is necessary to get state-of-the-art musical instruments up and running. Even the drums are powered by electricity.

The afternoon shadows lengthened as the grandstand filled to capacity. The concert began. Now things really got frantic as Da Yooper Traveling Comedy Show shifted into gear. Literally everyone in the entire troupe got into the act. Yooper truck drivers, sales people, and yes, even the sound engineer cavorted onstage in wigs, dresses, and costumes of assorted forest critters. Have you ever seen a bear dancing with a deer? Or a trout ballet? Da Yoopers have all of this, and I thoroughly enjoyed every minute. It was predictably entertaining, wacky, and often spicy, featuring a few songs whose verses would never make it into this newspaper.

The following day, the mood during the bus ride home was subdued. Some guys slept. Jimmy DeCaire continued working on his new song. Others shared special moments from last night's concert while sipping coffee, Coca-Cola, and even water (never once did I see any of them slugging down cans of beer—Da Yooper style). Motorists passing Da Yooper caravan honked and waved when they spotted the logo on the sides of the vehicles. The band members always waved back.

Before we left for Marshfield, I'd considered taking my guitar along just in case they wanted me to join them on some of their songs. A ridiculously naive thought. These people are dedicated, professional musicians, light years beyond me in skill. Maybe next year though, they might let me audition for a walk-on part as one of those dancing trout.

CRUISING: A HIATUS FROM REALITY

If you've wondered why you haven't seen my Sunday columns lately, it's because every now and then I get this overwhelming urge to vacation on one of those luxury cruise ships. I've just returned from a three-week-long voyage in the Pacific, visiting Alaska, Japan, Russia, South Korea, and China.

Cruising is the ultimate in high-on-the-hog travel: no battling your way up to the airport car-rental counter, struggling with unwieldy road maps as you inch along through congested traffic on the interstates, or wrestling your luggage in and out of motels. You simply stroll up the gangway onto this enormous, twelve-story, gleaming white ship where you're greeted by a crewperson so friendly that he has to restrain himself from hugging you. You're escorted to your stateroom where your baggage has already been safely delivered. A smiling room steward points out all of the stateroom amenities, presents you with a personal cruise ID card, and lastly states (every other word he utters is "sir") that if there's any little thing you need, just press the button located on the headboard of your bed. After you unpack it's time just to lay back and relax, perhaps sip a glass or two of chilled champagne, and look forward to waking up in a different country every morning.

You quickly find out that while you're elsewhere on the ship, the room steward sneaks in and makes your bed, vacuums, cleans the bathroom, replenishes the ice cubes in the refrigerator, puts fresh fruit in the bowl on the credenza, and tidies up all of the little souvenir knickknacks that you bought in the last port of call. And he does all of this *twice* a day.

All of your food is included in the cruise fare, and believe me, food is not in short supply. Beginning with early-bird coffee and danish at 6 AM, breakfast is served in at least three different locations throughout the ship for the next four hours. If that isn't enough, the pizzeria opens at midmorning to tide over any passengers feeling faint from hunger. This goes on all day long, winding up with a lavish evening buffet lasting well past midnight. And there's 24-hour room service for the truly desperate. Many people quite naturally take advantage of this extraordinary bargain and religiously participate in each and every one of these eating events. Cruise ships sit lower in the water at the end of the voyage due to the increased tonnage of the passengers.

Money isn't used on board a cruise ship. Nightly floor shows with live orchestras, dancers, magicians, and comedians are included at no extra cost, as are first-run movies, lectures, and classes on everything from line dancing to napkin folding (I've tried both, and line dancing is easier). Whatever else you need or desire can be had by merely whipping out your cruise ID card. You can wander into any of the fancy on-board boutiques and get clothing ranging from T-shirts to tuxedos with this card. The same applies to expensive jewelry, name-brand perfumes, designer watches, pricey lithographs at the art auction, or having any vintage French merlot or California cabernet wine delivered to your dinner table. Your ID will even get you chips at the ship's casino.

Too good to last? Well, of course it is. On the morning of disembarkation the warm aura of hospitality exuded by the members of the ship's staff is suddenly replaced by no-nonsense efficiency. They have to get you off the ship as quickly as possible to make room for the next boatload of passengers scheduled to be spoiled rotten.

A fat white envelope is slipped under your stateroom door. It contains two yards of computer printout, a detailed compilation of the charges that you accumulated while on board ship, rudely jogging your memory of the goodies and services that you selected using your ID card. There's the Calvin Klein all-weather reversible jacket that you couldn't do without during the glacier watch on the Alaskan coast. And the night you stared out the forward-facing windows of the Crow's Nest cocktail lounge, helping the captain steer the ship as you signed for six vodka martinis. Or the 14KT gold cruise ship replica tie clip that you had to have for one of the formal dinners. And how about the irresistible Russian lacquered box you discovered that will no doubt come in handy some day? Finally, there's the new suitcase which was necessary to hold all of the other stuff that you bought.

Then you're directed to vacate your stateroom and sit in one of the public areas to await further instructions for leaving the ship. The atmosphere has definitely changed. The crew who had graciously welcomed you aboard, weeks before, hurry by, far too busy to even smile. There is no last-minute shopping, gambling, or cocktails, because everything's closed and besides, your ID card is now a worthless piece of paper. Terse messages blare out from the public address system, paging delinquent passengers by name (letting everyone on the ship know who the deadbeats are) to hurry down to the purser's office to settle up their accounts. Finally, you waddle down the gangway, reentering the real world, financially wounded, and idly wondering why your pants suddenly don't fit anymore.

But cheer up. In a matter of weeks your mailbox will once again be crammed full of friendly cruise brochures, gaily advertising the upcoming exciting 1999 voyages. By the time you've whittled off the excess blubber put on by the marathon eating and saved enough money to make a down payment on the next cruise, you'll only remember the good stuff.

LIVING IN BED

I'm writing this lying flat on my back in bed with my laptop computer perched on my stomach. No, I'm not suffering from terminal laziness. I've got a bad back problem.

"It appears that you have a herniated disk," the doctor announced after probing my leg, jabbing it with a needle in numerous spots, and then bashing my kneecaps and ankles with his little rubber hammer.

"What's a herniated disk?" I asked.

The doctor went on to explain that back vertebrae are separated by disks. These disks, acting like cushions, flatten out with age, and once in a while bulge out like an old rubber tire with a weak spot. When that happens, you have a herniated disk.

This bulge frequently impinges on nerves that go to your back or legs, producing intense pain—in my case in the left leg. I first noticed it one day out on the golf driving range, and all summer long I thought I'd pulled a hamstring. It ached when I sat and kept getting worse, so I finally went to the doctor.

Standing and walking are okay, but for the past week or so I haven't been able to sit. Think of everything you do that requires sitting—driving or riding in a car, eating, travelling by plane, working at a PC, visiting friends. And don't forget the one thing that you absolutely *have* to sit for (it involves air freshener). I don't waste any more time than necessary in the bathroom these days.

I had to get down to Green Bay for a quick-response MRI scan to verify the doctor's diagnosis, and since I couldn't drive or even ride in a car without experiencing agonizing pain, my friend Jeff Jacobs came to the rescue. He put the rear seats down in his Cherokee, laid out a sleeping bag and a few pillows, carefully loaded me into the back, and took me down to St. Mary's Hospital in Green Bay. Truckers pulling up next to us at stop lights shot puzzled looks at this bearded guy laying flat on his back in the rear of the Cherokee, staring at the inside of the roof. Waitresses in the roadside restaurants nervously watched as I stood beside Jeff's table, eating my sandwich and drinking coffee. They were waiting for me to make a run for it without paying the bill.

Surgery is still very much an option, but right now the doctor is suggesting complete bed rest. Taking his advice, I'm staying in bed and doing everything right there. I eat three meals a day in bed. Eating in bed is very tricky because I can't sit up without pain. I've got my head propped up on two pillows, but even so, when I bring up a spoonful of food I have to carefully steer it over its target—my mouth. Until my aim gets better, a lot of it falls into my beard and mustache. Toast should be easy, right? I was eating a piece when it slipped out of my hand and landed—buttered side down, of course—on my shirt. I go through a lot of shirts these days. And then the inevitable happened; I spilled a full mug of coffee all over the bed. I opened the window to let the bed dry and retired to the living room floor for the rest of the day.

Spilled coffee notwithstanding, you don't want to see my bed. I sleep on one side, but the other side looks like a garage sale. I try to keep everything within easy reach: i.e., the telephone, phone directory, a book manuscript that I'm rewriting, my large unabridged Webster's dictionary, *Roget's Thesaurus*, various pieces of mail that I haven't yet filed away, a box of Kleenex, magazines and books, and the television guide. The other day the TV remote control sank to the bottom of this mess, and I thought I was going to have to make it without the morning news.

Invariably it seems that everything I need is down at the foot of the bed, and reaching for it really causes pain. So I've gotten handy at picking things up with my toes and dragging them toward me.

I'm also watching a lot more TV these days. It used to be that I'd check the early morning news and then turn the TV off for the day. Now I keep it on. Have you seen what they've got on daytime TV? I've *got* to get out of this bed.

Fortunately, I'm getting a lot of help from my friends and family. My cousin Barb Engstrom and her husband Al have graciously kept me supplied with groceries. Every few days I crawl into the back of Jeff's Cherokee and assume my prone position, and he takes me to doctor's appointments and the pharmacy. I suggested to Jeff that it would be nice to have a small refrigerator and coffee maker back there, but he wasn't too receptive. Please don't send over any chicken soup. My bed is in bad enough shape now.

CHRISTMAS TREES BACK THEN

The other day I was at Shopko, fending off vicious elbow checks thrown by frenzied Christmas shoppers hunting for Barbies, Furbies, and Beanie Babies, when something caught my eye. They had Christmas-tree icicles for sale. Remember years ago when everyone decorated their Christmas trees with tinsel icicles?

I furtively reached into the cardboard box and gave one of the icicle strands an experimental yank. It didn't break. Must have been made of mylar or something, not like the old ones.

When I was a kid in Ishpeming in the 1940's, the holiday season at our house officially began with the cutting of the tree. Back then, artificial Christmas trees didn't exist; furthermore, there weren't even any Christmas-tree lots in the U.P. After all, why on earth would anyone pay good money for a tree when all you had to do was walk into the woods and chop one down?

It was my father's job to go out and cut the tree. Shortly after Thanksgiving he would write a letter to my Uncle Hugo in Republic (no one had a telephone) cajoling him into driving to Ishpeming in mid-December. Hugo was our only relative who owned a car, and the old man needed his '37 Ford to get our Christmas tree hauled out of the woods.

When my uncle arrived, the old man would shoulder his double-bladed axe, grab a length of clothesline for tying the tree to the front fender of Hugo's car, and head out the door.

"Don't bring back such a big one this time," my mother would call after him.

Her words always fell on deaf ears. The old man figured that if you could get something for nothing you might as well get a big one. He would return home, triumphantly dragging a twelve-foot tree into the house. Then he'd attempt to stand it up in the living room only to have the top four feet bend over against the ceiling, jamming spruce sap into the filigree-design ceiling paper that my mother had so laboriously scrubbed during her spring cleaning.

"Take that thing outside and cut it in half!" she'd yell.

Finally, with the tree properly shortened and a wooden stand in the shape of an X nailed to the bottom, my father would put it in its usual place in the northeast corner of the living room. The frigid north wind whistling through the numerous cracks in our old, wood-frame house kept that corner a good fifteen to twenty degrees colder than the rest of the room, and my father reasoned that the Christmas tree would last longer there.

Then the real work began: trimming the tree. A huge cardboard box of Christmas decorations was retrieved from somewhere in the upper recesses of the house. Nesting in the top of the box, like a tightly coiled ball of snakes, were strings of Christmas-tree lights. The old man would pick them up and try to separate them.

"Who th'hell dumped these in here like this?" he demanded to know.

"You did, last January," my mother would reply.

When the lights were finally unsnarled, the old man would plug the strings together and wind them around the tree, pushing each light into an aesthetically pleasing position, then carefully clipping it to a nearby branch. This done, he would call us into the living room to witness the tree lighting. The lights would be plugged into the lone living-room electrical wall outlet, already seriously overloaded with a floor lamp and our large, megawatt, wooden floor-model Zenith radio.

You guessed it—nothing happened.

Every year the old man would stare at the dead strings of lights in disbelief, and every year he had the same response.

"*@!!##*@!&*##@!"

My mother would quickly usher me out of the room, but the damage was done. I'd already committed the words to memory.

One of the Christmas-tree light bulbs was always burned out, knocking out the whole string in the primitive series circuit. But—and this was where the fun came in—you never knew which one it was. The old man would spend the remainder of the day lacing the air with ripe profanity as he reached into the tree, unscrewing and replacing each light bulb to track down the culprit.

When at last the lights were fully operational, my mother would take over and hang the vast assortment of glass ornaments bought at Newberry's many years before. After that it was my job to put on the icicles.

The old icicles were fragile, made of tinfoil, and thin as a spider web. It required a surgeon's touch to handle them. Before placing each icicle on the tree, it had to be held and delicately stroked downward between thumb and forefinger to remove the wrinkles so it would hang straight. This was a laborious two-day job.

The final task was placing yards of white tissue paper under the tree, arranging it like new-fallen snow. Our Christmas tree was ready.

After supper that night, my father would turn out all the lights in the house and plug in the Christmas-tree lights. The tinfoil icicles would burst into a thousand colored points of light from the glowing red, green, yellow, and blue bulbs. Tiny sparkling tree images were projected all over the room—on the frost-laced front-window pane, the large glass dial on the Zenith radio, and the cellophane covering the shade on the floor lamp. Even the drab wallpaper took on a rosy glow. For hours I would gaze at the Christmas tree in silent awe, soaking up the sight and smell. I knew it wouldn't be there very long. In a matter of days the tree would be unceremoniously stripped of its lights, ornaments, and icicles (my mother made me carefully take them off to save for next year) and be cast out into the alley along with the torn wrapping paper, broken cardboard boxes, and other flotsam of Christmas. But on that night, and a few nights to follow, the tree was there to make Christmas a very special experience. And it always was.

INSECTICIDE FOR
THE MILLENNIUM BUG

I don't want to unduly alarm you, but January 2000 is only one year away, and it's time to give some thought to the Year 2000 computer problem—a.k.a. the Millennium Bug. Experts are predicting that on January 1, 2000, many computers worldwide will go bonkers because the machines can't tell the difference between the year 2000 and 1900. Here's a few things that could happen:

Children born on January 1, 2000, might begin receiving Social Security checks on January 3rd when a computer at the Department of Health and Human Services calculates that these kids are 100 years old.

An airliner experiences a Millennium-Bug hiccup in its navigational system causing the automatic pilot to steer a planeload of sun-seeking Midwesterners to Reykjavik, Iceland, instead of Miami, Florida.

Aunt Sophie programs her VCR to record "The Sound of Music" on the Family Channel but instead gets the feature-length, uncut version of "Bimbos on Death Row."

Okay, I made those up, but real problems are already occurring. True story: A customer in a gourmet-food store in Warren, Michigan, tried to pay with a credit card that was perfectly valid but happened to have an expiration date in the year 2000, causing the store's ten computerized cash registers to lock shut for half a day. Fifteen months later, computer glitches continue to plague the store.

Quite naturally, people are concerned about the Millennium Bug and its impact on the world's infrastructure. Will the global stock markets crash? Will ICBM's be launched accidentally? No one knows. Estimates are that hundreds of billions of dollars will ultimately have to be spent on high-priced computer programmers to fix the problem.

I have a confession to make. Please don't send hate mail, but I helped create the Millennium Bug.

That's right; back in the 1950's and '60's I programmed computers at aerospace companies out in California. I and thousands of other prehistoric nerds planted the initial seed of the computer mess that we're facing right now. Here's how it all happened.

In their infancy, computers had one basic way of receiving data from the outside world—IBM cards. Remember those? Each of the eighty columns on the card accommodated only a single-digit number or an alphabetic letter. Card space was at a premium.

Therefore, to save space, every time programmers had to input the year into a computer we used only the two righthandmost digits. After all, why punch in a 1-9-6-3 for the year 1963 when a 6-3 would do the job quite nicely in half the columns. The computer was programmed to know exactly what was meant and automatically added 1900. This practice became universally accepted and was soon used on every computer. Unfortunately, it was propagated onto succeeding generations of machines where space on IBM cards was no longer an issue, simply because programmers found it easier to rehost old programs rather than rewrite them for the new computers.

So now we've got tons of computers—no one knows how many— that work just fine between the years 1900 and 1999 but might act like nitwits in the new millennium because they think the year 2000 is 1900. No one ever accused computer programmers of being great planners.

But I have a solution.

Who do you think is most qualified to fix this problem? Those young, fuzzy-faced computer geeks who wear gold rings in various body parts and weren't even born when the problem was created? Absolutely not. Go right to the source of the problem, my generation—the people who screwed things up in the first place.

There are thousands of old programmers—I know a lot of them—who are now on Social Security and spend their days whacking weeds off the lawn or pushing shopping carts behind their wives in the supermarket. Would these people like to get back into the work force to save the world from certain chaos? You better believe it.

The federal government and large corporations should mount a vigorous recruiting campaign to find and hire these retired computer people. Newspaper ads would specify that people under sixty years of age need not apply. Old-time programmers would sign up in droves and do a wonderful job since computer programming is like riding a bicycle—you never forget how. They would quickly be able to isolate and fix the problem code. After all, they're the ones who wrote it. And the oldsters would work for peanuts because a big salary would jeopardize their Social Security income.

So that's my plan. If it's implemented, the Millennium Bug will soon be eradicated, and we'll all be able to enjoy a safe and sane new century.

❀ ❀ ❀

OUT ON A LIMB:
PREDICTIONS FOR 1999

Now that I've successfully implemented all of my 1998 New Year's resolutions and have no remaining vices left to deal with, I'll give you my New Year's predictions for 1999.

I predict that President Clinton's impeachment trial will continue in the Senate chambers throughout 1999, breaking the old record set by the first O.J. Simpson trial. As the trial wears on, CNN ratings of the live coverage will falter and then plummet while Clinton's presidential ratings continue to soar. As the year ends, Larry Flynt, publisher of *Hustler* magazine—at a cost of some 100 million dollars—will have purchased the testimony of a sufficient number of paramours to embarrass each of the one-hundred members of the Senate who are trying the President.

I predict that the annual U.P. road repair activity will, as usual, not begin until late September, at which time fifty thousand people will be hired as flag persons and every piece of road-repair equipment will be pressed into service to repair potholes in twelve thousand miles of Upper Peninsula roadway, thereby forcing everyone to stay at home until Thanksgiving.

I predict that the opening of the Sawyer airport will be delayed due to potholes in the runway which cannot be scheduled for repair until late October.

I predict that the United States will attack Saddam Hussein at least three times in 1999. The usual full TV war coverage will be brought to you by CNN from the rooftop of the beautiful downtown Bagdad Hilton. At the conclusion of each three-day war, the Pentagon will claim significant damage to all targeted military installations, with no civilian casualties. The Iraqis will broadcast their usual video clips of damaged hospitals, schools, and nursing homes. And the Iraqi wars will produce such successful TV ratings that Ted Turner will begin negotiations with the U.S. Defense Department and Saddam Hussein to make the wars a four-part mini-series in the year 2000.

I predict that my Pentium computer—purchased in mid 1998 for a large sum of money—will be considered totally obsolete and virtually worthless by mid 1999. I still won't understand Windows95 by the time that Windows98 becomes the standard operating system.

Here are a few stories that you might see in the *Mining Journal* in 1999.

Marquette High School has changed their logo from the Redmen to the Beavers. However, controversy is expected since it was discovered that, in protest of the new logo, several trees on the school campus have been gnawed down by unknown parties.

Microsoft dealt the computer industry another crushing setback when they recently took out a patent on the numbers zero and one.

Predictions concerning the Y2K problem:

—There will be plenty of open seating, with rock-bottom prices, on any airline you care to travel on during New Year's Eve.

—Over five thousand people will suffer cardiac arrests while climbing skyscraper stairs instead of using elevators.

—At the supermarkets there will be an unprecedented run on bottled water and beer.

—Due to Y2K glitches in their guidance systems, United States

Cruise missiles will actually begin hitting strategic Iraqi military targets, much to the surprise of everyone.

I predict that in April the Chicago Cubs—the team that I've adored and rooted for since I was twelve—will get off to a fast start. Sammy Sosa will blast several homers over the ivy-covered brick walls in Wrigley Field to take an early lead in the home-run race. Then in late August, teams like the Florida Marlins and the Arizona Diamondbacks will start sweeping series after series from the Cubs. The Cubs bullpen will begin surrendering four or five runs in the ninth inning with alarming regularity. At the end of the season the Cubs will wind up in fourth or fifth place, thus once more restoring my faith in their unique ability to maintain the underdog position that they've so successfully defended for the past fifty-three years.

I predict that after the University of Minnesota football team suffers another humiliating loss to Michigan in the Little Brown Jug game, Minnesota governor Jesse Ventura will personally invite Michigan Governor Engler to step onto neutral ground (Wisconsin) to settle the whole thing mano a mano.

I predict that by the end of 1999 I still won't know what rack and pinion steering is.

A VALENTINE'S DAY STORY

Back in the 1940's I toiled my way through reading, arithmetic, and the Palmer Method at Central School in Ishpeming. That was bad enough, but every February I had to suffer through another ordeal: Valentine's Day.

First, the teacher would inform the class when Valentine's Day was approaching—more a command than an announcement. Every kid knew the drill. We had to go out and buy valentines for our classmates.

The kid's valentines in the big bin at Newberry's five and dime weren't large or fancy, measuring only about three or four inches square and costing a penny apiece. There were lots of different kinds, and you had to be very careful. Some had Dick and Jane on the front, staring at each other with sappy expressions, with cute little verses inside, like:

> "I liked this valentine so well,
> I bought it just for you.
> There is no other playmate,
> I'd rather give it to."

Idiot stuff like that was okay for sending to girls, but you'd never give one of those to your buddies. You might get your brains scrambled by an ice-covered snowball. For pals, the more caustic variety of valentine was appropriate:

"Roses are red, pine trees are green.
You've got a shape like a jellybean."

After we'd purchased our valentines, signed them, and written the recipient's names on the small white envelopes, we had to turn them in to the teacher. She collected them in a big white cardboard box covered with red hearts. On Valentine's Day, the teacher would empty the box on her desk and divide the contents between three designated girl students. These girls, acting like playful postmen, would go up and down the aisles, delivering the valentines to the rest of us.

Ideally, every kid should have given a valentine to each of his twenty-five or so classmates. However, most of us didn't have that kind of money (a quarter was a whopping big sum in those days), so we only sent valentines to our friends and, of course, attractive members of the opposite sex. As you might imagine, Valentine's Day got pretty tense because some kids got more valentines than others. Naturally everyone kept careful count. The number of valentines you received was a direct measure of your social standing.

I hated Valentine's Day. I was chubby, not particularly good looking, and painfully shy. I was also shorter than most of the girls. My heart pounded with terror every time I counted those stupid valentines, knowing full well that the kid stuck with the lowest count could be ruined for life.

When I got to the fourth grade there was a girl who sat at the desk in front of me who was truly a goddess. She had saucy, flashing brown eyes, thick dark braids that coiled around her head like a halo, and a pert, freckled nose. Like many of the girls, she was taller than I was, and for a time I'd seriously considered keeping my galoshes on throughout the whole school year to cut down on her height advantage. I'd been smitten by this girl ever since the first day of school in September, but I didn't know what to do. I tried the standard courtship procedure for fourth-grade boys—poking her in the back with my pencil—but she only turned and glared at me.

On the day that our teacher made the Valentine's Day announcement, I said to myself, Yeah! This is it! The ideal time to make my move. I had to give this girl a *special* valentine. After school I rushed down to Newberry's where, with sweaty paws, I hastily shuffled through the pile of valentines in the bin.

Nothing! There wasn't a single kid's valentine suitable for this beautiful girl. Desperate, I began looking at the adult valentines, costing a nickel, and some even a dime. Many used words I didn't even know, and in fact, some of those grownup heartfelt verses were truly scary to a fourth grader. Finally I realized that if I got her a mushy valentine, she'd just turn around and laugh at me, probably show it to her girl friends. I certainly didn't need more pressure on Valentine's Day. I settled on an innocuous Dick and Jane specimen with a milquetoast verse. I'd copped out.

V-Day arrived and as the valentines were being passed out, I kept my head down. My stomach gurgled morosely in anticipation of another marginally low valentine count.

One of the teacher's little postmen dropped a valentine on my desk. It was from the girl in front of me. I ripped the envelope open. The valentine was a cutout of a circus clown juggling big red hearts. The caption read, "Stop juggling hearts—BE MY VALENTINE!"

Three of the hearts hovering in mid-air above the clown's head contained the words I-LOVE-YOU.

"How many did'ja get?" It was one of my pals standing next to my desk.

"What?"

She sent me a valentine that said I LOVE YOU. Omigawd, omigawd, omigawd, omigawd . . .

"How many valentines did'ja get?" he asked again.

I grinned idiotically. "Uh . . . I dunno. I didn't count 'em."

"Ya didn' *count* 'em? Whaddayamean ya didn't count em?"

"No, I didn't," I said, staring at the beautiful dark braids in front of me. Somehow, counting valentines wasn't important anymore.

BILL BUFFEY'S LAST HURRAH

The other day I was reading John Grisham's novel, *The Testament*. In one scene the protagonist was flying over Wyoming, scattering the ashes of a deceased billionaire from the open door of the airplane. Grisham wrote the scene as smooth and uneventful, after all, how difficult could it be to scatter someone's ashes? Well, let me tell you a true story.

A few years ago I was planning an Alaskan vacation cruise out of Vancouver, and I called my cousin Karen—one of my book editors—and invited her to go along. Karen was, at that time, committed to twenty-four-hour caregiving to her elderly mother and hadn't had a vacation in years. She readily accepted, planning to have her husband Ron take over the caregiving duties. A few days later she called me back.

"Is it okay if I take my dad along on the cruise?" she asked.

"Your dad? He's been dead for nineteen years," I said uneasily, not knowing where the conversation was going. Karen's father, Bill Buffey, has long been a family legend. He was a hard-drinking, handsome Irishman who drove fast cars and used his charming gift of gab to win over the old Finn women in our clan. Right up to the end Bill loved life and savored every minute of it.

"I have his ashes," Karen said. "For many years, when he and mother vacationed in the Pacific Northwest, Daddy used to go salmon fishing. He loved the area. His wish was to be cremated and have his ashes scattered over the water up there. I'll never get a better chance to do it than from this ship."

"I don't know if a cruise ship will let you do that," I told her.

"I'll put his ashes into my suitcase, and we'll ask when we get on board."

Twenty-four hours out of Vancouver, the 675-foot-long Golden Princess was steaming north off the British Colombia coast, just south of the protective islands of Alaska's inland passage. The Pacific Ocean was having its way with the large ship, giving it an unsettling rolling and pitching motion. It became even more apparent while we were having dinner in the large dining room.

I had been really surprised that the purser's office on board ship agreed to allow Karen to release Uncle Bill's ashes. With stipulations, however. It had to be done from the aft end of the Promenade Deck after dark so as not to disturb the other passengers, and there had to be a ship's officer in attendance.

After we finished dinner Karen brought out the ashes which were packaged in a shoebox-size cardboard box. The time had arrived. Still dressed in our formal dinner attire, we stepped out onto the Promenade Deck. Karen carefully cradled the box in her arms.

The heavy seas had been only a minor distraction while we were enjoying the comfort of the ship's dining room, but out on deck it was an entirely different story. The stiff, cold wind was whipping up large, angry waves that thundered against the ship's hull. Salt spray washed the teak decks. Off the aft end of the Promenade Deck where the ashes were to be released, the seas towered overhead like a dark mountain of water chasing the ship.

Karen struggled to remain upright on her high heels and finally held the box out to me. "Here, you do it."

I nodded and took the box from her. No big deal. After all, it was a simple task, right? While Karen and the ship's deck officer—a wide-eyed Filipino gentleman—looked on, I carefully made my way to the aft end of the rolling deck, carrying Bill's ashes. Bracing myself against the deck railing, I struggled to open the box. The crematorium had sealed it tightly. When I finally managed to tear the box open I found that the ashes were also securely sealed in a heavy plastic bag that wouldn't tear. I was getting cold and wet by now, so I clamped the edge of the bag between my teeth and ripped it open.

But the ashes weren't nice and soft like ashes are supposed to be. They were fused together into a single petrified piece. I tried breaking the piece up, but it was like attacking a cinder block barehanded. I asked myself later why I hadn't just pitched the whole thing over the side, but at the time it seemed the only proper thing to do was scatter the ashes over the water.

At last the ashes began to break apart, and I grabbed a handful and tossed them out over the churning water behind the ship. But the devilish wind currents whipped the fragments high into the air, swirled them around like a tornado, and fired them back onto the Promenade Deck, pelting my now thoroughly salty and soggy dark-blue suit. I moved down the railing to find a better launching point. This time I reared back and threw the ashes overhand trying for more distance. Again they soared high, spun around, and blew back to the deck, now peppering Karen in her black formal gown and the deck officer in his crisp white uniform.

Breathing hard now, and in final desperation, I leaned over the railing and unceremoniously dropped the remaining ashes straight down into the water. They splashed and sank without further incident.

"Can you believe that?" I said to Karen, wiping my face and trying to straighten out my windblown hair.

"Yes I can," she replied calmly, tears glistening in her eyes. "That would have been Daddy's style. He couldn't have planned it any better himself."

Bill Buffey went to his final resting place—the spot he'd wanted—but getting him there was not a simple task.

DOG-PADDLING THE INTERNET

I t's been seven months since I got my new computer and nervously stuck my toe into that gigantic seething whirlpool of information called the Internet. I haven't yet reached the status of a net surfer; I'm more of a dog-paddler.

But I do e-mail now, not because I think e-mail is all that great, but I have friends who *do* think it's that great, so I respond to peer pressure, spending more and more time answering e-mail. It's like receiving Christmas cards; you feel obligated to answer. People who, in the past, never ever bothered to write a letter or call, send me e-mail. I don't get it. To me, typing is still work. Sometimes when I get an e-mail I just answer with a phone call; it's a lot less trouble. I can still talk faster than I can type.

E-mail messages can be like chain letters (the internetters call it chain mail). Some guy up the line gets an e-mail that he thinks the whole world should know about, so he forwards copies to all his friends—and then they forward it to all their friends. I get a lot of those, but I don't forward them on. Someone has to put a stop to it.

E-mail has its uses, though. People send me jokes, and I always appreciate that. And if dancing reindeer or singing sunflowers are your style, then you'll enjoy electronic greeting cards. You punch in your name, a personal message, the recipient's e-mail address, and fire it off into cyberspace. They're free, so what the heck.

Web sites abound for things you could never imagine. Want to meet tiddlywinks enthusiasts? How about swapping trash talk with TV wrestling fans; accurate spelling is not a prerequisite. You can join a chat group of Ku Klux Klan members—yes, they have a web site—scary, eh? Interested in breeding elk? The North American Elk Breeders Association has a home page. There's another web site where you can learn how to insult people in French. You can join on-line clubs for marijuana advocators, second wives, Larry Flynt supporters, and Ozzie and Harriet lovers. There's also a club called "Save the Pigs." These people aren't pork lovers; they just think pigs are cute.

If you're a weather buff, you'll love the Internet. Want to find a place where the winter weather is worse than the U.P.? With a few mouse clicks you can get the five-day forecast for Irkutsk, Siberia. Actually, I just now brought up the Irkutsk weather on the net, and it's about the same as Marquette.

Hypochondriacs can find descriptions for a rich assortment of diseases that they think they might have. I won't go into the details of why I know this.

When I was working out in California, I spent many a lunch hour playing hearts. The other day I discovered games on the Internet, and digging a little further I found over a thousand people playing hearts on the net. People with handles: Psychobob, Fancypanties, Rasputin, Shadylady, Pothead, Nudedude, Suckerpunch, and some that I can't mention in a family newspaper. Why are all these people playing cards at two in the afternoon? Don't they have anything better to do? Well, I sat in on a few games—purely research, you understand—to see if I could find some answers. I won a few, lost a few, and then just watched for awhile. But then a curious thing happened. Players looking to fill up a table saw my name, (you have to log in to watch or play) and I began getting invitations. Messages were jumping onto my screen, like: "Queen Kong has invited you to play at Table 28. Would you like to join?" Queen Kong? Is that a man or a woman? Maybe it's a very large female gorilla sitting at her PC in a rain forest in Uganda who hates to lose at hearts. I declined.

I like the Internet for several reasons. For example, you can now fill out electronic forms and deliver them through the net. I filled one out and mouse-clicked it off to get a Library of Congress number for my new book. The only trouble was a few days later I was awakened at two in the morning by my computer telling me that I had mail. An electronic robot e-mailer who obviously never sleeps—and doesn't care who *is* sleeping—had just sent me my new book number imbedded in a hearty congratulatory message. This was from the Library of Congress in Washington, D.C.! Is our government being taken over by Internet software robots? I suppose, if you consider the way things have been going in Washington lately, it could be worse.

Well, I have to go now. Fancypanties and Shadylady may be in the Internet hearts lounge looking for a game.

THIS WAS NOT LITTLE LEAGUE

Spring has arrived and if you know me at all, you'd know that my thoughts are turning, not to love, but to baseball. As a kid in Ishpeming, I couldn't wait for the start of baseball season. As soon as the snowbanks melted down sufficiently, I was out there in the backyard, loosening up by firing an old tennis ball against the woodshed and fielding the ground balls that skittered through the mud and slush.

The kids in my neighborhood had to make do with whatever broken-down baseball equipment they had. The ball constantly got refurbished with fresh electrical tape to keep the cover on it. Bats likewise were taped since each and every one had at least one crack. Few of us had gloves, and the ones we did have were in tough shape, requiring frequent repadding with rags. There was no such thing as batting helmets—your head was on its own—and none of us owned a catcher's mask or a chest protector. Our ball diamond was right in the middle of South Second Street down by the LS&I railroad tracks Street lights and parked cars were designated as bases, and we had to halt the game whenever the occasional automobile drove through the infield. This would not be mistaken for Little League.

In spite of my love for baseball, I was actually pretty rotten at it. I shut my eyes and cringed whenever a line drive was hit in my direction, and you could see a foot of daylight between the ball and the bat when I swung at a pitch. We would choose up sides—the two biggest kids were the self-appointed team managers—and I was always the last to be picked. I'd be assigned to play right field, or what passed for right field on Second Street. Nothing was ever hit to right field, so I couldn't do much damage.

When I was twelve, my sister Esther, who was much older, took me to a Tigers' game at Detroit's Briggs Stadium. The Tigers were playing the Cleveland Indians that day, and Bob Feller was pitching for the Indians. Before the game started, Feller was warming up in the foul area in right field. I ran through the stands to get a closer look. Feller was kicking his left leg high in the air and firing his fastball which hit the catcher's mitt with a sound like a rifle shot. Never in a million years did I think that anyone could throw a baseball that hard. And those were just *warmup* pitches. When Feller was out on the mound during the game, I followed the pitches by the sound coming from the catcher's mitt, because I couldn't see the ball being thrown to home plate. But Hank Greenberg got a home run for the Tigers off of a Feller fast ball. How could Greenberg hit that ball over the wall—a ball I couldn't even *see*? I knew right then and there that I'd never become a baseball player.

So accepting the fact that I was destined to be just a baseball fan and not a player, I began following the Detroit Tigers. In the spring I would hurry home from school to catch the late innings on the radio since all the games were played during the day.

Harry Heilmann, an old Tiger hall-of-famer, used to broadcast the games back then. His deep, commanding voice added suspense to every grounder and fly ball. It was especially tricky for Harry when the Tigers played road games, because the team couldn't afford to take him along. Heilmann would sit in the Tigers' home office somewhere in Detroit and read the play-by-play action coming over the teletype.

He would say, "And here's Newhouser's pitch . . ." A long pause would follow while Harry read the next message to find out what happened to the pitch. Then, "IT'S A DEEP FLY BALL!" Harry would yell, trying to compensate for the absence of crowd noise in the teletype room Another long pause . . . and then he would add excitedly, "Greenberg races back to the wall and catches it for the third out!" No one could put high drama into a teletype message the way Harry Heilmann could.

So I've been an avid baseball fan for over sixty years. Baseball spring training is underway now, meaning that it won't be long before I can once again turn on WGN-TV and start agonizing over the slippery fortunes of the Chicago Cubs, a team I've been rooting for these many decades. Will Sammy Sosa crank out over 60 home runs again? Who knows? Will Kevin Tapini, an Escanaba native who won 19 games for the Cubs last season be able to reach 20 in 1999? I hope so. Maybe, I tell myself, the Cubs will even go all the way and get to the World Series this year. Surrre! I've been saying that for fifty years.

NEW-CAR FEVER?
NOT ON YOUR LIFE

A couple of weeks ago I went to the Superior Dome Auto Show with my old friend Jeff Jacobs. I go to the same auto show every year with Jeff, and every year he looks at the new Cadillacs and thoughtfully fingers his checkbook. Jeff already owns a Cadillac, but it's got nineteen thousand miles on it and he hates driving a used car.

We wandered over to a '99 Cadillac DeVille on display, and I casually glanced at the sticker price on the window. Forty-four thousand dollars! I laughed hysterically just as I do every year when I look at sticker prices. Jeff edged away from me, not wanting people to think that he was with me.

I don't believe in shelling out big money for new cars. Why buy something that loses half its value in two years? Most of the cars that I've owned have been, shall we say, well broken in. They're certainly a lot less expensive, plus it's been my experience that a used car adds a certain aura of excitement to the driving experience.

My first car was a 1930 Model A Ford that cost me ninety dollars of hard-earned soda-jerking money when I was in high school. I dearly loved that old jalopy, even though it had a few eccentricities. For example, Model A's were notorious for having wheels roll right off the car while you were driving. It happened to me once. Do you what it's like to stop a car that's got only three wheels? The last fifty feet are bumpy as hell. Then there was the problem with the front bumper. It was fastened on with two bolts, and occasionally one would come loose, dropping that end of the bumper onto the roadway where it would immediately wedge itself beneath the front wheel with a horrible, grinding, screeching sound, sending the car veering toward the ditch. There were several wide cracks in the wooden floorboards that I couldn't seem to keep patched. Whenever I'd drive through a mud puddle, my passenger—frequently a date—and I would get bathed with muddy water and steam from the hot muffler. But aside from those minor inconveniences, it was a good old car.

My second car was a 1950 Chevrolet that I bought during my college days at the University of Michigan. It cost five hundred dollars—pretty steep, right?—but the car only had twenty-seven thousand miles on it, so it was a good investment. Student cars on campus were rare in those days, and any guy who had one—even if he looked like Quasimodo—had a big social advantage over his pedestrian counterparts. I had no trouble getting dates after I bought that car—in fact, that's how I met my first wife. Come to think of it, maybe buying the Chevy wasn't such a good investment after all.

When I was living in California—married to the girl that I picked up in college with the '50 Chevy—we didn't have a lot of money, so I was driving a '47 DeSoto (remember those?). It had a state-of-the-art fluid-drive transmission that would think long and hard before moving the car after you put your foot on the gas pedal. That wasn't its only problem. The wiring behind the dash would occasionally burst into flames, and I finally resorted to driving around with a seltzer bottle. I divorced the wife and the DeSoto at about the same time.

Single once again, I acquired a 1956 MG Magnette sedan, an elegant little machine with a genuine walnut dashboard—the perfect auto for a young, mobile bachelor in the 1960's. Unfortunately, after awhile the MG began to develop a perplexing problem. The engine would cough and then quit but only after being driven on the L.A. freeways for at least fifteen minutes. Several high-priced British mechanics with Richard Burton accents couldn't pinpoint the problem. The car ran like a charm on the city streets but would cough fitfully and come to a stop on the freeways. This is most inconvenient in Los Angeles, so I finally waxed the MG to a pearl-like finish, polished up the walnut dashboard, and brought it in to a Nash dealer to trade in on a new 1963 Rambler.

The dealer looked the MG over. "How's it run?"

"It runs great," I replied enthusiastically. "Why don't you take it for a spin around the block?" I crossed my fingers, praying that he wouldn't take it out on the nearby San Diego Freeway. Fortunately he didn't, and we negotiated the trade. Thereafter, I decided never to buy a used car from a private party. Trying to unload a car will turn anyone—including me—into an unscrupulous, conniving crook.

The 1963 Nash Rambler—the only new car I've ever bought—was a real lemon. I'm convinced that a bunch of highly intoxicated assembly workers swept up the floor at the Rambler plant and found enough miscellaneous parts to build one last car. When I got it home I discovered that one of the hubcaps didn't match the other three and the upholstery in the back seat wasn't a match with the front. The brakes had an annoying squeal, and the windshield wipers only worked when it wasn't raining. It took me three months to completely debug that car. I finally got rid of it about the time I acquired my first house and my second wife. She was a dedicated house remodeler and convinced me that what we really needed was a pickup truck to haul the gallons of paint, rolls of wallpaper, and the other assorted decorating materials that would ultimately keep us in the poorhouse for years to come.

After owning a couple of pickups, I bought a used 1988 Oldsmobile, and I'm still driving it. It runs fine, except that I keep hearing disturbing little knocks and squeaks indicating that the car is getting a little long in the tooth. One of these days I'll have to bite the bullet and get another vehicle. Does anyone know of a two- or three-year-old car, well-maintained with less than twenty-thousand miles, that's for sale? I know this sounds extravagant, but it *is* the '90's, and . . . well . . . I'll go as high as three thousand dollars.

WANNA BUY SOME GOOD STUFF?

I don't move very often—three times in the last twenty-three years—but I just moved into a new apartment. I hate moving with a passion, but this time I had no choice; I found the perfect place.

I spotted an ad in the *Mining Journal*: "Magnificent two-bedroom apartment in East Marquette historical mansion. 1500 square feet. Spectacular view of Lake Superior." The owner showed me the apartment early the following morning. The sun's reflection off the lake bathed the ten-foot, beamed ceiling in the huge living room with warm, cheerful light. I wrote out a check right on the spot.

For those of you who've forgotten the sheer joy of moving, let's review the drill: first, you get your hands on a thousand cardboard boxes and pack up sixteen tons of your worldly possessions, then hire a crew of burly men, whom you've never met before, to load the boxes, your priceless antique furniture, and big-screen TV onto a large truck with out-of-state license plates. Finally, you mail out enough change-of-address cards to alert half the population of the United States.

But this move shouldn't be too bad, I reasoned. After all, I'd disassembled and saved all of the cardboard boxes that I used when I'd moved from California. I'll just use them again.

I began to pack. In two days the boxes were filled. I went to

Office Max and bought twenty more. A few days later, I went back for another ten. And ten more the following day. It suddenly dawned on me that I've collected a lot of stuff over the years. I could understand it if I were married with children, but I'm a bachelor and bachelors aren't supposed to have that much stuff. Of course, it's all very useful, potentially valuable, or has a deep sentimental attachment. Like the hand-held, battery-operated TV set that comes in handy when the power goes out during California earthquakes. And the thousands of 35mm slides from every trip I've taken since 1960. There's the collection of National Geographics that I know will be worth a tidy sum one day. From my mother I inherited (maybe collecting stuff is genetic) a large box filled with marriage, baptism, and confirmation certificates dating back to the early part of the century, not to mention my old grade-school report cards. I couldn't possibly throw those treasures away.

The movers—two husky lads in their twenties—arrived promptly at eight-thirty in the morning. They nodded their heads agreeably—or so I thought—as I explained what had to be done. I left them to get started on the job while I delivered a carload of the more fragile items— lamp shades, guitars, and the like—to the new apartment.

At times I've been known to embellish facts, but what happened next is absolutely true. When I returned, the moving van was gone, but all of my belongings and furniture were still sitting there in my old apartment. I called the moving company and got hold of the manager.

"I really must apologize," she said. "One of the fellows who showed up at your place this morning quit ten minutes later."

"He quit? Why?"

"Remember that we gave you an estimate of six hours? He called me and said there was no way that the two of them could move you in six hours. 'There's just too much stuff,' he said."

"So he just walked off the job?"

The manager replied, "Well, actually, he quit the company."

"He quit the company because of my *stuff*?" I couldn't believe it. I knew I had accumulated a lot of possessions, but when movers begin quitting after they lay their eyes on it . . . well . . . maybe I should seek professional counseling.

"Look, I'll see if I can get two more fellows to come out there to get this move done," the manager said.

She lined up another pair of movers who arrived at my old apartment at two-thirty. Nigel and Bill didn't seem to think there would be any problem moving my stuff.

"No sweat," said Nigel, the smaller of the two, as he snatched up three stacked boxes filled with books—easily weighing over a hundred pounds—and scurried out to the van.

By 9 PM the move was complete. Nigel and Bill had done an outstanding job, getting everything into my new apartment without so much as a scratch on any of my belongings. But the next morning I surveyed my elegant new home with dismay. My glorious view of Lake Superior was now eclipsed by mountains of cardboard boxes in the living room.

For the past several days I've been diligently unpacking. Fortunately, the new apartment has generous storage space—twenty-eight cupboards in the kitchen alone. But here's the scary part. I'm filling it all up. What am I going to do a few years from now when my stuff begins to overflow all of those cupboards, closets and drawers? Move again? I don't think so. Maybe I'll hold a garage sale. Anybody out there in the market for some good stuff?

❂ ❂ ❂

WHO'S IN CHARGE, ANYWAY?

I had to call one of those megacompanies to notify them of my change of address. A sweet, friendly voice—a computer, what else?—answered, saying, "Thank you for calling XYZ Company." The computer proceeded to give me a series of menu options so lengthy that by the time it was finished I'd almost forgotten why I'd called. Naturally, none of the options was for making a change of address, but finally the computer tempted me by saying, "To speak to a customer representative, press six." I pressed six, and the computer tauntingly informed me that, "All of our customer representatives are currently busy, but please hold . . ." The computer piped syrupy music into my ear for the next ten minutes until it finally realized that it needed the phone line to annoy another human and kissed me off with a dial tone.

Another morning recently, I was suffering through the weekly chore of grocery shopping at the supermarket, placing groceries on the moving belt at the checkout station. The checker ran my box of All Bran over the scanner and then stared at the cash-register screen, puzzled. She picked up one of my low-fat cherry yogurts and tried to scan it in, still puzzled.

"Something wrong?" I asked.

"They put a new computer system in yesterday, and now it's not registering the items. Let's try another station."

We moved to an adjacent cash register, but the same problem occurred. The computerized cash register didn't want to add up my groceries. By now there were several people standing in line behind me with full carts, and the enormity of the problem was becoming abundantly clear to the checker. She quickly got on the paging system and called all personnel to the front of the store. Grabbing stuff from my cart she assigned several items to each of the stock boys who then raced down the aisles to find the prices and report back. After a lengthy period of time, all of the groceries in my cart were hand-tallied and I paid up and headed for the door. By now the store manager was on the phone, talking frantically to some computer technician. Stock boys and assistant managers were running insanely around the store searching for prices. The checkout lines were filled with irate customers. It wasn't a pretty sight.

Just last week the first printing of my latest book, "Cold Cash," was scheduled to roll off the presses at BookCrafters, a downstate printer. I called my BookCrafter's coordinator person to check on the status of the books.

"We've got a serious problem down here," she said. "Last night, during a thunderstorm, the plant was struck by lightning."

I almost dropped the phone. "Omigawd, my books—did they burn up?"

"No, nothing like that, but the resulting power surge affected some of our computers. I can't access the status of your production job."

I said, "Well, can't you just go back into the production area and see if my books are done?"

"I wouldn't even know where to look. The computer assigns a printing press to each incoming job, but it doesn't tell me which one. When the job is finished, the production foreman keys in the completion status at his terminal and the computer updates my data base. I never have to go back there."

"What are you going to do?" I asked, concerned since I'd told bookstores that my book would be available within a week.

"I'm not sure. The whole plant is at a standstill right now. They've called in computer technicians. I'll have to call you back."

Fortunately, BookCrafters somehow resolved the problem and my books were located, but these incidents are begging the question, "Who's in charge here, anyway?"

The answer is, the computers are, that's who. No matter where you go, computers are running everything: telephones, cash registers, automobiles, gasoline pumps, wrist watches, and—gawd help us travellers—airplanes. Computers keep track of our money, and if there's any suspicion that one of them isn't doing a good job of it, another computer jumps in to check up on the first one. Your car is chock full of computers which—whenever the mood strikes them—will flash obscenely bright lights in your face, informing you how you're screwing up.

People blindly obey computers nowadays, and the computers know this and have become quite snotty and overbearing. In fact, they take time off, only working when they feel like it. And people can't do much about it either, because everyone's forgotten how to do things by hand, like adding and subtracting or keeping track of things.

I suppose computers—when they're running—do things faster, cheaper, and more accurately, but I can't help but think back to the days when telephones were answered by humans, and the only lights on your car were the headlights and taillights. Cash registers didn't require electricity and operated with a big hand crank on the side. Grocery clerks had all of the prices memorized. You had to wind your alarm clock. People knew how to multiply and divide using a pencil and paper. It seemed to me that we always got to where we wanted to go, knew how much money we had in the bank, and received the right change. It's unfortunate that we can't go back to those days again. Then the only Y2K problem we'd have would be remembering what year to write on our checks.

ARE YOU FEELING OLD YET?

I borrowed the theme for this column from an item I saw on the Internet, and I think it's appropriate for the graduation season.

Last month I delivered the keynote address at the Republic High School commencement exercise. I immediately noticed that the graduating seniors were very young-looking. I certainly never looked that young when I was in high school. Then it struck home. These kids were born in 1981!

1981! Galloping generation gaps! I've never known anyone who was born in 1981. All of my friends and relatives were born in the 1920's, '30's, or '40's, and I'm giving a few of my aunts and uncles a break here.

These young people who will be entering college this fall have no meaningful memory of presidents other than Bill Clinton and possibly George Bush. To them, the Great Depression occurred on Black Monday in October 1987. The Korean and Vietnam wars are ancient history, as is Neil Armstrong stepping on the moon. Three Mile Island and Watergate also happened years before they were born. They've never known the threat of nuclear war.

For them, postage stamps have always cost over thirty cents. They've never seen an airmail stamp. Cars have always had power steering and brakes. They've never had a gas-station attendant check the tire pressure and oil when they stopped to fill up. They've never seen a Packard, DeSoto, or a Hudson. They have no idea what Route 66 is or where it went.

They can't imagine a world without computers, but they probably have no idea what IBM cards are. VCR's and CD players have been around all of their lives, but on the other hand, they're unfamiliar with the term 8-Track. The expression "you sound like a broken record" means nothing to them because they've never owned a record player. They know a lot about video games, but they've never played Pac Man or Donkey Kong.

They would be surprised if you told them that Washington, D.C., once had a baseball team and all of the games were played during the day. They wouldn't have the foggiest notion who the St. Louis Browns were. These kids weren't around when the Boston Celtics were really good. They wouldn't have any idea who Cassius Clay is and have never heard of Seattle Slew.

Their kitchens have always had microwave ovens and electric can openers. Most of them have never seen black and white television or a set with only thirteen channels, and they've never watched "Laugh In," "Have Gun Will Travel," "Charlie's Angels," or "Twilight Zone." They don't know who J.R. was and don't care who shot him. Many of them are not familiar with the names Alan Ladd, Doris Day, Dick Powell, or Gordon McRay. Elizabeth Taylor and Mickey Rooney are old people, and Richard Dreyfus has always been bald. They've never seen an action movie where the f-word isn't used.

Automatic teller machines, digital clocks, answering machines, and remote controls have always been part of the daily lives of these young folks. A pen that has to be filled with ink would be a curiosity. They've only seen milk in plastic and cardboard cartons, and powdered creamer is an everyday thing. They can't imagine a lawn mower without an engine. Running shoes have always naturally had velcro closures.

They would think it incredible if you told them that at one time girls had to wear dresses to school—every day. They also wouldn't believe that in the same era teachers thought nothing of it when you carried a pocket knife into the classroom but would smack you silly for anything else. They might laugh if you told them that only women wore earrings and only men got tattoos. They'd think it really quaint that baseball caps were worn to shade the eyes and not the back of the neck.

These young people have never heard of Decoration Day or Armistice Day. They're also unaware that Washington's Birthday and Lincoln's Birthday used to be two separate holidays. They don't know who Patricia Hearst is, and they may never have heard Neil Diamond. As far as they're concerned, Wal-Mart has always been around. The chances are, they've never ridden on a train.

So there you are. These young adults, born in 1981 and the leaders of tomorrow, will be in college this fall. Are you feeling old?

THE SUMMER OF '48

I was visiting my Aunt Imbie and Uncle Arvid at their remote riverfront home on the Michigamme River near Republic. While we were having coffee, Imbie handed me an old ledger with frayed binding, yellowed pages, and half the cover missing.

"Your Aunt Elma found this among your mother's personal effects," she said. "You might find it interesting."

I did indeed. The ledger, dated 1948, had been kept by my mother while operating the Dairy Bar, a small three-booth diner in Republic. Detailed bookkeeping entries for expenses and income were logged daily into the old ledger in my mother's precise handwriting. It was fascinating reading. At the time milk was seventeen cents a quart. Buttermilk, even cheaper at twelve cents a quart. A loaf of bread cost fourteen cents. The restaurant rent, sixty-eight dollars a month.

It had been my mother's lifelong dream to have her own restaurant, and she had excellent credentials, having worked in the kitchens of two posh private country clubs in Milwaukee during World War II. One problem with my mother's new restaurant: she wanted to draft me into a summer job as the soda jerk.

"It's not like I'm asking you to do it for nothing," she said. "I'll pay you five dollars a week."

"Why me?" I argued. The last thing I wanted that summer was a job in a restaurant. At age fifteen I'd just finished my freshman year at Republic High School, and I needed some serious time to think about serious things—girls, in particular. The girls in my class had suddenly sprouted all sorts of curves and bumps and were talking about things that didn't make any sense at all. Even my pals—guys who only last summer were by my side killing rats at the town dump—were now casually tossing around cryptic phrases like "making out." These new developments scared me silly. That summer I just wanted to be by myself and do some leisurely fishing on the Michigamme while I mentally sorted out this disturbing turn of events.

But my mother insisted. I had no choice but to begin learning the fine art of soda-jerking: properly blending a malted milk with the electric mixer, memorizing the ingredients in a banana split, spritzing the exact amount of carbonated water into a chocolate soda to get that fresh fluffy dome on the top of the glass.

Somewhere my old man had gotten hold of a secondhand juke box—a mean-looking machine already way past its prime in 1948. It was a five-foot-high Wurlitzer with sweeping laminated wooden sides well scarred from long-forgotten barroom brawls.

And it kept breaking down. The old man, who was never a mechanical genius anyway, would peer into the back of the monster, scratch his head, and shrug. Finally, I pulled up a chair behind the Wurlitzer, studied the jungle of gears, levers, and wires, and after much trial and error got it running again. So in addition to soda jerking I became the de-facto juke-box repairman. Whenever it broke down I fixed it. I must have used up all of my mechanical proficiency on that damned Wurlitzer because after that I was never able to fix anything.

The juke box turned out to be a real moneymaker, but it used 78 rpm records and they quickly wore out. I frequently had to hitchhike down to Ishpeming—the big city—to buy new ones. This was important because the music I selected had a direct impact on our juke-box profits. In fact, that summer we made a fortune on Frankie Yankovic's "Blue Skirt Waltz." It was the favorite of the grizzled old pulp cutters who came to town on weekend binges. Between drinking bouts at the local bars they'd lurch over to the restaurant to eat, and pump an endless stream of nickels into the Wurlitzer to hear Frankie Yankovic and his golden accordion. After weeks of hearing the "Blue Skirt Waltz" my mother grew quite tired of Frankie Yankovic. She said that if he ever walked into the Dairy Bar, she'd break all of his fingers with the potato masher so he'd never play the accordion again.

My mother prepared only one entree each day, and it was always one of the three basic M's—meatballs, meat loaf, or mojakka (moy'ah'ka), the Finnish stew that many of you are perhaps overly familiar with.

One day, shortly after we had opened for business, a large batch of mojakka was bubbling merrily away in the pressure cooker. Suddenly, with a horrific blast, the valve on the heavy pressure cooker cover gave way, and in a microsecond the cooker emptied, sending a supersonic stream of potatoes, carrots, celery, onions, and beef shooting upward to stick fast to the Dairy Bar ceiling. For days afterward everyone in town was talking about the big mojakka explosion at the Dairy Bar. When you lived in Republic back in the '40's, anything was news.

One afternoon a girl I knew from high school came into the Dairy Bar and ordered a chocolate malt. She was, without a doubt, the cutest girl in the entire town, and I'd never had enough nerve to even talk to her. The situation called for decisive action. Using an extra scoop of ice cream I whipped up an ultra-thick malt for her. It must have been good because the next day she returned with some of her girlfriends. By now I was fairly skilled at soda jerking and decided to put on a clinic. Nonchalantly tossing the metal malt can into the air, I caught it with the other hand and with dazzling speed and wrist action fired in three scoops of ice cream. The girls watched in awe as I held the quart milk bottle high in the air and splashed in the milk like a white waterfall. Then I punched in a generous dollop of chocolate syrup, added a pinch of malt, and with a spinning body flourish jammed the can up onto the mixer, cranking up the chocolate malt with a mighty roar.

From then on there was a steady stream of high-school cuties coming in to get their thick chocolate malts and to watch the show. I loved it. It didn't matter that I had a raging case of acne and tripped over my adolescent tongue. The Dairy Bar was my stage, and I was the main act.

The Dairy Bar is gone now. Only a gigantic hole remains where Cleveland Cliffs put in an open-pit mine in the 1960's, but I'll always keep fond memories of the Dairy Bar and that wonderful summer of '48.

DECISION-MAKING AT THE SUPERMARKET

I was trudging through the supermarket the other day, doing the weekly grocery shopping, and noticed that toilet paper was on my list. I wheeled the cart over to the toilet-paper shelf, and suddenly the huge array of different brands caused me to suffer a "senior moment." I couldn't remember what kind of toilet paper I use. There were a zillion different brands on the shelf. One claimed to have 560 single-ply sheets per roll, another—more expensive—400 double-ply sheets per roll. Many of them advertised even more mathematically challenging statistics—462 square feet, or if you prefer the metric system, 42.9 square meters. You can buy ultra soft, super absorbent, patterned, quilted, rippled, or toilet paper made of 100% pure cotton. Cotton? Is it washable? And toilet paper is packaged in many different sizes—single roll, two rolls, four rolls, six rolls, twelve rolls, and the twenty-four-roll economy size, large enough to require a pickup truck to haul it home.

I still didn't have the foggiest idea which brand I use, but I grabbed one at random and proceeded on. But now I was curious. I toured the supermarket, inspecting the wealth of choice of other merchandise. Toilet paper has no monopoly on large selection.

On a hot summer day you may feel thirsty and walk into a supermarket to buy some beer. I did a count—drawing suspicious glances from other shoppers since it took awhile. There are two hundred and sixty-three choices available to the beer buyer. Aside from the popular American brands, there's beer made in Mexico, Germany, Canada, Japan, Holland, England, Ireland, and Australia. You can drink light, premium, extra pale, dark ale, cream ale, Scotch ale, pilsner, genuine draft, bock beer, Irish amber, honey porter, and something called woodchuck draft cider. You can get your beer in sixteen-ounce cans, twenty-four-ounce cans, regular sixteen-ounce bottles, long-neck bottles, or quarts, all available in six-packs, twelve-packs, a case of twenty-four, or if you're *really* thirsty, a thirty-pack, assuming you're strong enough to get it into the car.

I counted one hundred and seven different kinds of toothpaste. Crest alone features labels like Multi-care, Gum Care, Tartar Protection, Cavity Protection, Sensitivity Protection, Fresh Mint Gel, Extra Whitening, and Baking Soda and Peroxide. For the kids there's Barbie, Barney, and Star Wars toothpaste. I found nothing simply calling itself toothpaste.

Got a headache? It might get worse trying to pick out a painkiller. There's Advil, Nuprin, Motrin, Exedrin, Dristan, Tylenol, Nytol, Bufferin, Ibuprofen, Aspirin Free, and Vanquish, and those are just the well-known ones. Buried away in this tonnage of caplets, tablets, and gel caps, I was gratified to see good old Bayer Aspirin, although I don't know how they've managed to survive the onslaught of competition.

But first prize absolutely has to go to the breakfast-cereal industry. The cereal shelves run half the length of the store and hold two hundred and fifty-seven different varieties. Aside from the traditional, like Cornflakes, Grape-Nuts, Wheaties, and oatmeal, you can pour your milk into Apple Jacks, Mini-Wheats, Snack Abouts, Cocoa Krispies, Corn Pops, Marshmallow Mateys, Weetabix, Cookie Crisps, Cocoa Pebbles, Alpha Bits, Smacks, Crunch Berries, Toasty O's, and Marshmallow Blasted Froot Loops, just to name a few. Of course, many of these are also available with added raisins, apples, cinnamon, genuine wild blueberries (suuurre they are), peaches, almonds, dates, walnuts, and pecans. And if you really want to blast off with sugar-fueled mega-energy in the morning, there's Chocolate Chip Cookie cereal. If they'd had cereal like that when I was a kid, I'd have been wearing dentures by age eleven.

Why is there so much stuff in grocery stores these days? In the 1940's in Ishpeming—and Ishpeming isn't much bigger now—you could find everything you needed at the A&P on the corner of Cleveland and Second Streets, a store no bigger than a Tru-Value Hardware Store, which it now is. Six of those A&P's would fit in a present-day Econofoods store. But the A&P didn't need a lot of room because they didn't carry that many different brands. Bayer Aspirin was the only thing available for headaches. Colgate, Pepsodent, and maybe a few others were all the toothpastes you could find. If you didn't like Northern Tissue toilet paper, you had to resort to last year's Sears Roebuck catalog. There weren't many choices, but nobody seemed to mind. The only thing anyone worried about back then was scraping up enough money to buy what *was* available.

So are we better off with tartar-fighting, extra-whitening, sensitivity-protecting, fresh mint gel toothpaste? I don't know, but every time you shop, it takes five times longer that it should. And when you get your toothpaste home and are standing in the bathroom brushing your teeth, you're subconsciously wondering if you should have gotten one with more whitener, peroxide, or better gum protection. You're vaguely dissatisfied and don't even know why. Wouldn't you have been perfectly happy if the only toothpaste in the store was plain old white-paste Colgate?

I wonder if all of this decision-making isn't frying our brain cells. There are people in the supermarket slowly shuffling up and down the aisles, eyes glazed over, vainly trying to cope with the billions of brands, packages, and flavors. If we're not careful, we'll soon be a population of supermarket zombies.

I'll admit one thing, though. *Any* kind of toilet paper is better than the Sears Roebuck catalog, especially when you get down to the colored glossy pages.

IS ALL THIS PROGRESS NECESSARY?

I really don't understand many of our modern-technology developments.

Last April when I moved into my new apartment on Arch Street I discovered that the kitchen had a trash compactor. I'd known about trash compactors but had never operated one, being a long-time advocate of the jam-your-fist-in-the-can-to-mash-it-down technique. So I asked my landlady about its use.

"It's really quite simple," she said, opening the compactor drawer. "You just line this inside box with a tall Hefty kitchen bag, put your trash in, and press the switch."

It really *was* simple. I tossed in all of my trash—milk cartons, cans, paper plates, the whole works—and the trash compactor squashed it down just fine. Every so often I'd look in the drawer, but there was always plenty of room left, so week after week I kept chucking in the trash. Then one morning I noticed that the kitchen was getting, shall we say, a bit gamy. Maybe it's the trash compactor I thought, so I decided to empty it. I opened the drawer and attempted to pull out the Hefty bag. It wouldn't even budge. After repeated compression the plastic bag had fused itself to the inside of the metal drawer. I gave the bag a mighty tug. It jerked free, popped into the air, split open, and spewed one hundred and seventy-five pounds of very dense garbage all over the kitchen floor. The bottom trash was about two weeks away from turning into coal. This is progress? What's the point of compacting trash if you have to keep emptying the damned compactor all the time?

Shortly after I'd bought my Oldsmobile in California, I called a garage to inquire about an engine tuneup.

"Is it a V-8 or a V-6?" the mechanic asked me over the phone.

"It's a V-6," I replied after a long moment's hesitation. "At least I *think* it's a V-6. Wait a minute, maybe it's a V-8."

I could hear him breathing on the other end of the line, thinking that this phone conversation would make a good story during the afternoon coffee break with the other mechanics.

After hanging up I rushed out to the Oldsmobile, popped open the hood, and peered inside to see if I had a V-8 or a V-6. It was like looking into a huge tin of tightly packed sardines, except these sardines were made of rubber, metal, and advanced electronic equipment. I didn't recognize a thing. It was an ocean of wires, pulleys, and belts with a dozen different places to add fluids of one type or another. Not a square inch of room was left. An oddly shaped metal plate covering the engine read "Fuel Injection," indicating that there were no spark plugs. I was in trouble. Spark plugs had always been my sure-fire method for determining the number of cylinders an engine has. After prolonged inspection, I decided that the Olds was a V-6, although I still wouldn't wager any real money on it.

Now, why does a car need all of that junk crammed underneath the hood? If you just want a minor tuneup, it costs a fortune to disassemble and reassemble all of it. For years I drove a 1971 Chevy pickup truck and everything under the hood was plainly visible and identifiable. I could easily find the spark plugs, air cleaner, starter, generator, the master cylinder—everything.

My new computer is internetted to the extreme—ultra-fast and multi-tasking—and it works just fine, until you lose power during a thunderstorm. When the power comes back up, the computer has experienced extensive memory loss and begins to ask embarrassing questions about passwords that I don't have. It issues terse messages directing me at some length on how to proceed to get the machine back to some semblance of operational status. My user's manual has grown sweaty and dog-eared. I used to be able to shut down my old 486 PC anytime, and it came back up just fine without giving me a pop quiz on computer science.

And it's not just hardware things. A friend gave me a barbecue grill as an apartment-warming gift. Not a fancy one, but quite serviceable all the same. My apartment has a large porch overlooking Lake Superior, an ideal spot for leisurely dinners on warm summer evenings. I invited my curmudgeonly old buddy Jeff Jacobs over, telling him that we'd take my new barbecue grill out for a trial spin with a few choice filet mignons. The last time I'd grilled anything was back in 1984 out in California, but after all, how hard could it be to barbecue a couple of pieces of meat?

Just before Jeff arrived I dumped briquettes onto the grill, poured some charcoal lighter on them, and lit it with a match. They flamed up nicely, and I busied myself with other chores while they heated up. Except they didn't heat up. I gave them more time but the briquettes remained stone cold. Finally, I looked at the label on the briquette bag to see if I was doing something wrong. The label informed me that I'd bought ceramic briquettes.

"You tried to set fire to ceramic briquettes?" Jeff exclaimed when he arrived. "Ceramic briquettes are for gas grills. Didn't you say you had six years of college?"

"Ceramic briquettes?" I cried. "When did they invent those? And why?"

"I *knew* I should have eaten over at the Northwoods Club," Jeff muttered.

Writing about all of this is very depressing, and I'm getting a headache. I going to take an aspirin if I can get the hi-tech childproof cap off the bottle.

SO YOU WANT TO SEE
YOUR BOOK IN PRINT

As many of you know, I write books in addition to newspaper columns. Over the years, hundreds of unpublished authors have approached me at signings, wanting to know how to get their book into print. I'm dedicating this column to those unsung heroes and heroines of the written page.

There are two ways to get a book published. You can submit your manuscript to one or more book publishers—there are literally thousands of them around the country—to see if they're interested in your story. *Writer's Market*—an annual volume and an excellent investment—carries an extensive list of publishers, complete with their specialties and ground rules.

It should come as no surprise when I state that most publishers, for any number of reasons, will send you a politely worded rejection slip. A publisher's opinion of what's fit to put into print almost never coincides with your ideas or mine. And most publishers of any size will only look at manuscripts submitted through a recognized literary agent. Getting the attention of these agents is a monumental task in itself. However, don't let rejection slips discourage you from submitting to publisher after publisher. Patience is the watchword. Many writers have literally papered their walls with rejection slips.

Your other option is self-publishing. If you *REALLY, REALLY* want to see your book in print, then this should be a serious consideration. Self-publishing is taking on the responsibility for the design, manufacturing, marketing, and distribution of your book, much as an outside publisher would do. You are in control of your own destiny. *No one* tells you what to do because you do it all yourself. The Upper Peninsula Publishers and Authors Association (Tel 906-644-2598) is a superior resource for self-publishing. I'm a member.

When you're self-publishing, the fun really begins after you've completed the manuscript. First of all, application should be made for an International Standard Book Number (ISBN), similar to registering your car. While it's not totally necessary, most bookstores won't touch a book that doesn't have an ISBN. There's still more paperwork—a Library of Congress Catalog Card Number and a copyright.

Next comes the book cover. Unless you're an accomplished artist, you'll have to hire a graphic artist to design the cover. What colors should the cover and title lettering be? Colors are important because you want your book to catch the eye of the potential buyers. What goes on the back cover? A bar code, for one thing. Again, bookstores and book distributors don't want to handle books without bar codes.

Unless you're experienced with desktop-publishing computer software, you'll also need to hire someone to do the page layout—the detailed design of the pages, i.e., type style, line spacing, margin size, page placement, etc. The layout will determine precisely how many pages your book will have.

Now you're ready to talk to the printers–the folks who actually build your book. There are plenty of printing companies around, and it's a good idea to contact at least three or four of them because their quotes may vary substantially. Getting references is also a good idea since writers have been burned by unscrupulous printers.

The printer will ask about the weight and color of paper you want for the pages. (Getting complicated, isn't it?) You'll want white paper, but there are about fifty shades of white, some of them easier on the eyes than others. And how will the book be bound? Don't use wire spiral binding because the bookstores want the title showing on the spine when the book is stacked on the shelf. Those people are sticky about a lot of things.

Finally, the happy day arrives. The printer calls and announces that your books are printed and ready for shipment. Where would you like them delivered? I strongly urge you to have the storage problem well thought out in advance, since a printing of, say three thousand books, will easily take up a space the size of your bathroom. Many self-published authors have to park their car on the street because their garage is full of books.

When your books are safely stashed in the garage, under your bed, or disguised as a large coffee table in the living room, it's time to get them into the readers' hands. This is marketing and distribution. If at all possible, enter into an agreement with one or more book distributors—big wholesalers like Partners and Ingram. It's more paperwork, but they can help get your book into the retail outlets. I also recommend talking to Amazon.com and Barnesandnoble.com. They're the major on-line booksellers, and oddly enough, it's relatively easy to get them to carry your book because they both want to have every book on the planet in their inventory.

It's no time to be bashful when you're marketing your book. Knock on radio-station doors and get yourself invited onto their talk shows. Convince bookstore managers that you should do signings in their store. Get on the phone and call all of your friends and relatives or mail out postcards. Create a press release and fire it off to every newspaper in the state, graciously offering to give them a complementary copy of your book if they'll be kind enough to review it. And finally, load up the trunk of your car with cases of books and take off, hitting every whistle-stop store within a two-hundred-mile radius to convince them that their stock isn't complete without your book. I've done all of this, which is why my beard has turned gray.

Oh, and did I mention that all of this costs money? Be prepared to put up between seven and ten thousand dollars or more to have that load of books delivered to your house with no guarantee that you'll get your money back. It's certainly not easy, *BUT* . . . if you've really got a good book and you're willing to invest the money and time, you just might convince people to reach into their pocketbooks and buy it.

I know that all of this sounds mighty discouraging, but I'll leave you with one final thought. When you open up that first crate from the printer and pick up the top copy of your very own book, there's absolutely no feeling like the immense satisfaction and pride you'll get, knowing that you've given birth to the whole thing. It makes it all worthwhile.

VISIT HELSINKI, BRING MONEY

Lately I've scarfed up untold quantities of pickled herring, smoked salmon, Danish cheese, and lingonberry pie. The shops I've been in displayed endless racks of hand-knit Nordic ski sweaters, herds of plush stuffed reindeer, and armies of troll dolls. I've rubbed elbows with more Lutherans than one would ever expect to meet in a lifetime.

I've just returned from a Baltic cruise, touring the larger Northern European cities: Copenhagen, Oslo, Stockholm, Helsinki, St. Petersburg, and Tallin, Estonia. A tough job, but someone had to do it. Since I'm a Finnish American, I thought I'd share some of my observations on Helsinki.

When Yoopers claim that summer occurs on the Fourth of July, it's said with tongue in cheek. In Finland, it's true. The morning I arrived in Helsinki—16 August—the temperature was in the low fifties, not too bad, but it didn't get much warmer. Only a few weeks earlier the sandy beaches near the city were filled with sun-bronzed Finns. By mid-August they were deserted. Summer in Finland was over. In fact, school was starting on the day I arrived.

Finland has had a long history of lengthy occupation by other countries, yet current-day Helsinki—population 600,000—is a bustling, self-sufficient, beautiful city. With an innate artistry which seemingly runs contrary to their stern, sisu-like nature, the Finns have skillfully woven streets around and through dense groves of birch trees and rock-bluff outcroppings. Parks abound. Electric streetcars glide along the wide, clean downtown boulevards. There's moderate traffic congestion, but no horns honking or short tempers. Road rage is beneath the dignity of Helsinki drivers. Mannerheimintie, the major avenue, is most cosmopolitan with large, up-scale stores, including Stockman's, a Baltic replica of Harrod's in London.

Many people aren't aware that Finland is officially bilingual. Swedes occupied the country for so many centuries that both languages are commonly used, making the reading of Helsinki street signs, with fifteen-plus-letter Finnish and Swedish names, a tough task.

But it's actually quite easy to explore Helsinki because practically everyone speaks English. In fact, Finns speak a lot of languages. In addition to Finnish and Swedish, English and German are compulsory in the elementary schools.

Most Helsinki restaurants will provide you with an English-language menu on request. However, if you're still unsure of the food, there's plenty of McDonald's and Pizza Huts around to see you through. Visa, and Mastercard are widely accepted, even by the taxicab drivers. Many stores will also accept American money if you don't mind getting your change in Finnmarks.

Speaking of money, bring lots of it. At a small downtown cafe I had a modest lunch consisting of a smoked-salmon-and-cheese sandwich, a small piece of lingonberry pie, and a cup of coffee. The bill came to the equivalent of fourteen dollars. A cup of coffee costs two dollars, and if you want a refill, it's another dollar. One good thing, tipping is not expected.

At Stockman's—admittedly a pricey store—men's shirts go for about ninety dollars. Neckties are fifty. A plain-Jane, three-cushion sofa costs the equivalent of two thousand U.S. dollars.

In the city proper there are almost no single-family homes available, so the Finns buy apartments. Now we're talking *real* money. A cozy two-bedroom apartment (600-700 sq. ft.–I mean *small*) will set you back 800,000 to 1 million Finnmarks, or 150-200,000 U.S. dollars.

Taxes are stiff. Hard merchandise has a 22% value-added tax (VAT), driving up the price of clothing, furniture, housing, and automobiles. Even the churches (86% Lutheran) get into the tax act. The government nicks everyone's paycheck with a one-percent church tax. Books are tax exempt, though. Finns believe that literature is a necessity and should be available to all at minimum cost.

On a new automobile (all of them are imported) the import tax is an incredible 130%, driving the cost of an unadorned Chevy van well over $50,000 U.S. But you'd never buy a Chevy van anyway. Gasoline runs about four dollars a gallon, and only the most affluent motorists can afford to drive big cars with V-8 or V-6 engines.

With this very high cost of living, it's no small wonder that Finns ferry across the Gulf of Finland to Estonia to do their shopping.

But they endure. The economy is strong, unemployment is minimal, and they somehow managed to avoid becoming embroiled in the insanity of world politics.

These days Helsinki residents are sporting caps and T-shirts reading "Helsinki 450," advertising the city's four-hundred-and-fiftieth birthday in the year 2000. It's certain to be a festive celebration, and I can highly recommend the trip. Like I said though, bring lots of money.

STRIKING BACK AT TELEMARKETERS

The other evening I was at home, just sitting down to a hot dinner when the phone rang. If you're a bachelor, preparing any kind of a hot meal is a major production, and I didn't want to talk to anyone. But thinking it could be important, I answered the phone.

"Hello."

"Am I speaking to Mr. Gerald Har-joo?"

I ground my teeth. No one who really knows me calls me Mister or Gerald, and they certainly know how to pronounce my last name.

"Yes."

"Mr. Har-joo, my name is Tina Smedley. I represent Dewey Swindleham Banking Services Corporation, and we're proud to offer you our platinum VISA card . . ."

I interrupted. "I'm sorry, but I'm holding out for plutonium whenever it becomes available." I slammed the phone down and went back to my now lukewarm meal.

I imagine that this has happened to all of you on a frequent basis. Telemarketers are making everyone's life miserable these days, offering everything from credit cards, long-distance carriers, and magazine subscriptions to time-share condos in Puerto Rico.

So what can be done about these home invaders? Well, you could try an unlisted number, but it wouldn't really help. Telemarketers work from long lists of telephone numbers, and they couldn't care less if your name appears next to the number or not.

But I have a few ideas. You may not be able to stop telemarketers but you can certainly slow them down. Better yet, you can exact a certain amount of sweet revenge while performing a valuable service to all mankind.

Years ago, while I was still living in California, the phone rang one night. I'd just finished eating dinner and was idly wondering how to spend the rest of the evening. The answer to that dilemma was forthcoming.

"Is this Mr. Gerald Har-kewww?"

"Yes, it is."

"Good evening Mr. Har-kewww, my name is Brian Blabber of Salton Sea Paradise Acres. We'd like to offer you an all-expense-paid weekend trip to the lovely Salton Sea for both you and your wife. Congratulations sir!"

The Salton Sea is a murky body of water one hundred and fifty miles southeast of Los Angeles, smack dab in the middle of the California desert with scorching summertime temperatures rivaling Death Valley. It's perilously close to the San Andreas Fault, and many seismologists believe that's it's only a question of time before the BIG ONE hits, plunging the entire area—Salton Sea included—to the center of the earth. Not exactly a location where one should buy real estate. But I had time to kill that evening.

"That sounds wonderful," I said. "Tell me more."

Smelling a sale, the telemarketer became very enthusiastic. He explained how I'd receive free transportation in an air-conditioned bus directly to the Salton Sea Paradise Acres office, be shown a short half-hour video tape, and be given a free tour of one of the condominiums. Lunch would be included.

"A free lunch?" I exclaimed. "That's great!"

"Of course, you'll have to bring your wife," he said. "Any real-estate transaction that may take place will have to have the mutual consent of both parties. I'm sure you understand."

"My wife, huh? Well, I'll ask her. She might think it'd be fun. I'll be seeing her at the courthouse tomorrow morning."

"Courthouse?"

"Yes. She's taking me to court for skipping a few alimony payments. A silly misunderstanding, really. I told her that I'd make payments as soon as I found a job."

"You're not employed, sir?"

"Well, not right now. But I've got plenty of time. My unemployment doesn't run out for another week."

"Well, Mr. Har-kewww, it's been nice talking to you . . ."

"Wait, don't hang up," I cried. "I really need a condominium or something. I'm being evicted in two weeks . . ."

He hung up.

If the telemarketer is a woman and you're a guy, you might try this one.

"Mr. Gerald Har-agool? My name is Sara Goodbody at XYZ Telecommunications, and I want to tell you about our exciting, new Dial-a-Dime long-distance service . . ."

"Sara . . . what a pretty name. My third wife's name was Sara. Or was it my fourth wife? Of course, that's all ancient history now. I'm currently unattached. How about you?"

"Mr. Har-agool, let me explain about Dial-a-Dime . . ."

"Sara, with that sexy voice you can explain *anything* to me. Tell me, where are you calling from?"

"Uhhh . . . I'm in St. Louis."

"St. Louis? Right next door! I can catch the 9 PM flight out of here, make a quick connection in Chicago, and with the time-zone change be in St. Louis before the bars close. We could have a drink or two and get acquainted. What's your address, Sara? . . . Sara? . . . Are you still there? . . . Sara?"

Of course, there's always a certain element of risk associated with that ploy. Sara might not have much of a life and really like the idea. It would be disconcerting to be stalked by a love-starved, frumpy, middle-aged woman from St. Louis for the rest of your life.

There's always the geezer approach.

"Mr. Gerald Har-a-que? My name is Joel Jabberwocky, and I want to tell you about our new . . ."

"Kin ya speak up young feller? M'hearing aid fell inta the oatmeal this mornin' an' ain't been worth a damn since."

"HOW'S THAT, MR. HARA-A-QUE?"

"Better. Kin ya give me that name again?"

"Joel Jabberwocky, sir."

"Jabberwocky? Are you related to the Jabberwockys over in Newberry? I knew ol' man Jabberwocky back in the '30's . . . Hello? Hello? . . . Ya still there?"

So you see what can be accomplished, using a little imagination. If you can burn up ten minutes of a telemarketer's time, time that would otherwise be used aggravating several other innocent people, you'll be performing a major service to society.

UNDER THE KNIFE AND BACK

Everyone likes to talk about their operation, and I'm no exception.

For some time I've had a herniated disk in my lower back, and it's bothered me off and on. I wound up in Green Bay in the examining room of a young (to me, anyone under fifty is young) orthopedic surgeon who looked at the MRI's of my spine and without hesitation stated, "I can fix it." I liked his brash, confident style and decided to have him perform the surgery.

Having surgery is a complicated business, beginning with preregistration over the telephone. A woman from the Green Bay hospital called and kept me on the phone for thirty minutes with plenty of questions.

"You want to know about every pill I take?" I exclaimed. "It's a lot—doctor's prescriptions, herbal medicines, vitamins, aspirin, not to mention topical ointments."

"I have to know everything you put in your mouth and on your skin," she said.

After she had extracted my complete medical history and that of my family going back to ancestors in Finland, she gave me my pre-op marching orders. No aspirin during the week prior to surgery. No food or liquids after midnight the day before; your stomach must be completely empty before general anesthetic. My friend Jeff has his own theory; the real reason they don't want you to eat before the operation is so that when you finally get fed, you'll be so hungry that the hospital food will taste pretty good.

The morning of the surgery I checked into the hospital and was taken up to my room. A lab tech drew blood, and then I was shuttled around to different departments for x-rays and an EKG. Back in my room a nurse scrubbed my lower back and proceeded to mess up a perfectly clean bedsheet swabbing my back with Betadyne antiseptic.

The surgery was painless, as most are these days, and before I knew it, I was being wheeled back to my room in a high state of grogginess. That's when the problem began.

The nurses kept giving me ice water to drink, but a strange thing was happening. Nothing was coming out, even though I *really* had the urge to go. It seems that general anesthetic not only puts your brain to sleep; it puts your whole *body* to sleep. My plumbing had forgotten to wake up.

"We'll fix that," said one nurse and produced a lethal-looking catheter.

But it wouldn't go in.

"Hmmm. Do you have a prostate problem?" she asked.

I couldn't answer the question. I was too busy screaming.

"Don't worry," she said. "We've got a new advanced model for this type of problem." She brought out a different type of catheter, one with a curve on the end. That one felt even worse, but it worked.

Later on the catheter was removed, but all night long the nurses kept urging me to drink ice water to jar my bladder into action. While the situation was improving slightly, I soon had a full tank again. By now the nurses were carefully measuring how much liquid went in and how much was coming out. For convenience they kept the two jugs side by side on my bedside table. During the night I reached over to pour myself a drink of water and picked up the wrong jug by mistake but fortunately caught the error in the nick of time.

At 8 AM I told one of the nurses that it was time for me to take some of my pills.

She looked at me suspiciously. "You brought pills with you?"

I pointed to my bag on the chair and she took out my pills, all neatly arranged in daily plastic compartments.

"These pills aren't properly labelled," she said. "I'll have to lock them up in the narcotics cart."

"But they're nothing but a few prescriptions, vitamins, and herbal medicines," I argued.

The nurse looked at the medication list on my chart. "I can order all of them from the hospital pharmacy." She took my pills and hustled off to lock them up, returning later with duplicate pills in properly labelled containers.

And you wonder why medical insurance is so high.

It was time for breakfast. I hadn't had a thing to eat in a day and a half except for two mouthfuls of Jello, some apple juice, and four gallons of ice water, so when they brought me a tray I was pretty hungry. I eagerly scarfed up lukewarm oatmeal and scrambled eggs that resembled K rations from World War II. It was all delicious. Jeff was right. When you're hungry enough, anything tastes good.

Later that morning the surgeon came in to tell me that the operation was a success and that I could be discharged from the hospital. I mentioned my urination problem. He didn't think it was all that serious, but just to be on the safe side they decided to plug in one more catheter to drain me before the long trip back to Marquette. One for the road, so to speak.

Jeff had agreed to drive me home, and as he waited at the curb with his Jeep, a nurse pushed me out in a wheelchair—standard hospital procedure. Hospitals think nothing of sticking four catheters into you but wouldn't dream of letting you walk to the front door under your own power.

I'm home now, and everything is going well. I can take walks and drive short distances, but there are lots of rules to follow during my recovery. No bending over. Call me clumsy, but there isn't a day that goes by that I don't drop something on the floor. I just leave it there. Whenever friends come over and ask what they can do to help, I ask them to pick up a few dozen things lying around on the floor. I've got a girdle that has to be worn for six weeks. And thigh-high surgical stockings to prevent blood clots. The stockings are impossible to get on, but once on they begin sagging around my knees.

Well, it's time to wrap this up. Maybe I'll go over to Wal-Mart and try to find a masculine-looking garter belt to hold up these stupid stockings.

SOME ASSEMBLY REQUIRED

Late one Christmas Eve in Ishpeming, when I was four or five years old, I woke up to a loud commotion down in the living room. It must be Santa Claus, I thought. I jumped out of bed and rushed to the stairs to watch him at work. It wasn't Santa Claus though; it was my father trying to put a tricycle together. The air was blue with Bull Durham smoke as the old man, clenching a hand-rolled cigarette in his teeth, sat on the living room floor attempting to force the handlebars onto the tricycle frame. The air was also blue with words I'd never heard before. Spotting me crouching on the stairs, the old man took the cigarette out of his mouth and tried to explain that Santa Claus had been behind schedule and didn't have time to put the tricycle together.

It must be in the family genes because I absolutely hate to put things together. I've sworn at drawers that are supposed to fit into do-it-yourself desks. I've torn fingernails trying to screw legs onto coffee tables. I've inadvertently installed bookcase shelves upside down only to find that the underside was unfinished. Anything that comes disassembled in a cardboard box strikes terror in my heart.

I've tried to avoid buying things that aren't already put together, but I still get suckered in. One day I was prowling around in Shopko looking at lamps. I spotted a matching set on sale—a table lamp and a five-foot floor lamp. A nice design and the price was right. Naturally, you can't buy the store's display models—I believe it's a federal crime—so I hunted down a clerk. He gave me a box that measured no larger than fifteen inches by fifteen inches by a foot high.

"No, no, this can't be right," I told him. "I want that set of two lamps with the wide brown shades. One of them is a five-foot floor model. They can't possibly fit in a box this small."

"They're both in there, including the shades," the clerk assured me. "There's some assembly required."

Apprehensive, I brought the box home and carefully slit it open with an Exacto knife. It was packed tight with ingeniously sculpted chunks of packing foam that surrounded all of the parts.

Each piece of the two lamps was tucked away in a separate pocket of the packing foam and sealed in a bulletproof plastic bag. Included were two packets of desiccant silica gel; I suppose to keep the plastic bags nice and dry and hard to tear open.

The two lamp shades were nestled together tightly, each meticulously wrapped in miles of cellophane stripping. My mother always left the cellophane on lamp shades, and now I know why. It takes forever to get it off.

I unpacked the parts, screwed the various sections of the lamp pillars together, mounted the pillars into the bases, plugged the harps into the switch assemblies, and fastened on the shades. It took me over an hour to assemble the lamps and another fifteen minutes to sweep up the packing foam which is specially designed to crumble into sawdust-size pieces at the touch of a hand. To top it off, the lamps had five-foot cords. I have never found a wall outlet within five feet of where I want to put a lamp. Why can't the lamp manufacturers skip the fancy box and just give me an assembled lamp with a ten-foot cord?

But at least a lamp doesn't talk back, which is more than I can say for the home computer that I once tried to put together. You see ads in the paper all the time about how simple it is to run down to Wal-Mart, K-Mart, or Shopko and pick yourself up a computer, take it home, plug it in, and be on-line in a few hours. Don't believe a word of it. I ordered a brand-new 486 PC which arrived in three large cardboard boxes. When I opened up the boxes it became immediately apparent that there was some assembly required. There were millions of components: CPU, keyboard, mouse, speakers, monitor, printer, and they all had to be joined together with miles of weird-looking cables. After several days of reading through twelve inches of manuals, peering into twenty-seven-prong ports, and puzzling over a one-hundred-and four-key keyboard, I finally managed to get the whole thing hooked together. I flipped on the switch.

The computer was like a new-born baby. It didn't know a thing. It began asking me a slew of silly questions like, "What kind of printer do you have?"

"Whaddaya mean what kind of printer do I have?" I yelled at it. "I just mated you with the printer using that stupid cable that it took me an hour to find. What do you want, a personal introduction?" For years I yelled at that machine, and right up to the day I replaced it with another computer, it would ask me cryptic questions about itself, clearly indicating that I really hadn't put it together properly. Last year I had a local guru come to my apartment and assemble my latest computer. He estimated it would take him fifteen minutes to do the job. It took him half a day. That made me feel better.

In a way my old man's lucky he's not around today. I can just see him on Christmas Eve, trying to assemble a computer. He'd put a kitchen match to the instruction manuals, heave the machine into the nearest snowbank, and go shopping for a tricycle.

❂ ❂ ❂

I'M A YOOPER AGAIN

These days I'm going around saying "whah!" and "eh?" a lot, something I haven't done in a long while. It figures, though. I've been back in the U.P. three years now, and the vocabulary is coming back. I'm becoming a Yooper again.

Of course, during my childhood in Ishpeming and Republic I was a Yooper and didn't know it; the word hadn't been invented yet. Back then I thought people in the U.P. were just like anyone else. It's not true, of course. Yoopers are different, and I'm proud to become one again.

I think Yoopers are just plainly nice people. Now I'm in the habit of walking along the streets of Marquette, smiling at strangers, and saying "good morning." I never did that before. No one walks, much less smiles, in Los Angeles. If you stroll along a street out there, smiling and saying "good morning," you'd be turned in as a suspicious character and a possible pervert.

Most Yoopers don't rush around as if their lives depended on it. I know I've slowed down quite a bit since I've moved back. It's really changed my driving. All those years on the Los Angeles freeways, I'd clip along at seventy-five miles an hour, just keeping up with the bumper-to-bumper traffic. Most mornings I was already doing sixty pulling out of the parking structure.

So when I first moved back to Michigan, the police kept stopping me for speeding. I tried to explain that it was taking me a while to adjust to the slower pace, but for some reason the troopers weren't sympathetic. Now my driving is Yooperized. I peacefully wend my way along US-41 at a sedate fifty-five miles per hour, and I'm perfectly content to do so.

And I had to relearn how to stop the car. In California I thought nothing of slamming on the brakes, decelerating from supersonic speeds to a near-complete stop in order to swerve around overturned cement trucks, multiple rear-end collisions, and other common, everyday mishaps on the freeways. You can't do that up here. Slam on the brakes during a U.P. winter, and you'll whirl off into a mile-long skid and wind up in a cedar swamp, if you're lucky.

Yoopers are inherently honest, and it's easy to get in the habit of leaving your car unlocked. I know I do. Leave your car unlocked in California, and within twenty-four hours it'll be languishing on a back road outside of Tiajuana, Mexico, minus all of its moving parts.

Lifelong natives here don't realize what a luxury it is to pump gas without having to pay first. Los Angeles gas pumps are electronically locked until you slip money into the slot beneath the bulletproof shield at the cashier's booth. If you pull anything out of your pocket besides hard cash, the cashier will punch a hidden alarm and in minutes you'll be surrounded by a SWAT team.

And I love the news headlines up here. Where else can you find lead stories about a high-school logo or deer feeding? They may be debatable topics here, but these issues are much easier on the nerves than drive-by shootings, home-invasion robberies, and freeway pursuits.

I've really begun to enjoy the four seasons again, especially the fall colors in October. But Southern California isn't shortchanged on seasons. Those folks have four seasons too—fire, flood, mud, and smog. Do leaves turn color in California? I don't know. During October—California's smog season—you can't even *see* the leaves. I think I've heard them gasping for air, though. Maybe they turn blue.

So we get a little snow, so what? Digging out of a snowbank is easier than living in your car after your house falls into the Pacific Ocean during THE BIG ONE.

My blood pressure is lower now. My hiatal hernia doesn't bother me anymore. I've quit taking Pepto Bismol. I can even sit in my car at the road-repair sites, serenely waiting for the flagperson to let me pass without fighting the urge to blow my horn. I bought a new car a few months ago, and I'm not even sure if I know where the horn button *is*.

I'm not a full-fledged Yooper yet. There are still a few things left for me to do to qualify. I have to buy my camp, of course. And I still haven't acquired a taste for deep-fried fish on Friday nights. I'll work on it.

CHRISTMASES PAST:
TINKERTOYS AND TIDDLYWINKS

I can't help but wonder why children's toys have to be so hi-tech these days. I mean, does a kid really need a remote-controlled robot capable of launching missiles at the family cat? Or a talking doll with a brain so sophisticated that she reminds your daughter that her birthday is coming up? Personally, I feel that children can be amused and challenged quite nicely with more basic toys.

Between the ages of five and nine, my Christmas present of choice was a new box of Tinkertoys. Tinkertoys were nothing more than a collection of wooden spools with holes and quarter-inch-thick dowels in a variety of lengths. The dowels plugged into the spools, and presto, you had enough building blocks to construct anything on God's green earth. I built a replica of the Empire State Building, an Indy 500 racer, a Flying Tiger pursuit plane, and even a horse. There was always a blueprint in the Tinkertoys can for a whole host of things to build, but I largely ignored the plans, preferring to use my own imagination. If, by some quirk of good fortune, I happened to find two sets of Tinkertoys under the Christmas tree, so much the better. That gave me twice as much building material. In fact, a kid's social status was measured by the number of Tinkertoys sets that he owned.

My father loved games. My Christmas presents provided the old man with a perfect excuse to get down on the living-room rug and show off his skills. Tiddlywinks were his favorite. The game was simple in principle but next to impossible to play well. Tiddlywinks were played on the rug using a glass jar and several brightly colored, nickel-sized smooth disks which were the winks. The object of the game was to get a wink into the jar by pressing down on the edge with another wink, causing the first wink to pop into the air. Simple, right? Wrong. You had absolutely no idea where the wink would go. It could take a feeble little hop and go nowhere, or maybe fly off sideways under the sofa, or zoom straight up and hit you between the eyes. When my mother got down on the rug and tried her hand at it, even the dog took cover. It was a tough game, but my old man was the champion. He could put those winks into the jar with astonishing regularity, and I couldn't understand that because he never played it the rest of the year.

One of my favorite games was Pick Up Sticks, and we always had a fresh set at Christmas. There was a bundle of eighth-inch diameter sticks to a set, each one color-coded to denote its point value. To start the game, somebody held the bundle of sticks in his fist and then let them drop to the rug into a random pile. The trick was to extricate, one by one, the high-value sticks from the pile without disturbing the others. Pick Up Sticks required very steady nerves, which I had when I was a kid.

If you really wanted to get hi-tech in the early forties, you bought your kid a Gilbert's Chemistry Set. I got a set one Christmas. It was a collection of little glass bottles containing a splendid assortment of strange and exotic chemicals, small beakers, and a candle to brew up evil concoctions. Gilbert furnished an instruction book with detailed recipes for producing compounds with multi-colored smoke that would discolor the wallpaper and putrid odors that would drive your dog outdoors. But the only thing I was interested in was conjuring up something that would explode. Oddly enough, the manufacturer provided step-by-step instructions to do just that. I carefully followed the instructions, but the explosion was nothing but a wimpy little pop that didn't even get my mother's attention.

The most expensive Christmas present I ever got was a Lionel electric train. On Christmas morning I was excited and could hardly wait as the old man mounted the train tracks onto a piece of plywood. That done, we hauled it upstairs to my bedroom to play with it. But the novelty quickly wore off for me simply because there was only enough track to form a small oval, and there's only so much you can do with an electric train that goes round and round on an oval track. It was a different story with the old man, though; he loved that train. This was state-of-the-art technology in those days, and pretty soon all of my father's friends were trooping up the stairs to my room to take turns driving the train. It was weeks before the cigarette smoke cleared out.

I don't remember anything about my first two Christmases, but my mother once told me that I didn't get any presents at all. To keep me amused she put me on the floor with a big jar of buttons, and I'd sit there for hours on end sorting them out. I suppose I must have swallowed some of the buttons, but no one seemed to worry about things like that back then. Buttons for kids to play with would be totally unacceptable now. They'd be declared hazardous, and besides, buttons don't require batteries or computer chips.

REMEMBERING THE NINETIES

A few words should be said about this passing decade, the nineties. There were plenty of people who got their fair share of headlines in the nineties, and it would be okay with me if some of them didn't get any more. I'm referring to the likes of O.J. Simpson, Muammar Khadaffi, Sadam Hussein, Newt Gingrich, Monica Lewinsky, and sometime basketball professional Dennis Rodman, the 1990's fashion setter with his rainbow haircuts and multiple tattoos.

Fashion trends bring up some interesting questions. These twenty-something girls getting perky little butterflies tattooed on private areas—will they still be happy with their butterfly forty years from now when it's sagged into the shape of a bat? And how do you eat peanut butter with a ring in your tongue?

The 1990's saw young people paying all kinds of money for jeans with the knees torn out. When I was young and my jeans got that bad, I just threw them away. If I'd known that they were going to appreciate in value, I'd have kept them locked up in a safe.

Another '90's fashion trend: young guys going around with the sun visor on their baseball cap shading the back of their necks while wearing eighty-dollar sunglasses to keep the sun out of their eyes. Would someone please explain that?

One '90's apparel innovation that I really like is shoes with velcro straps. I have to confess that I'm not very good at tying my shoes. They frequently come untied, and when I give the laces a good tug to keep them tied, the bows wind up crooked and sad looking. With velcro straps you just mash 'em onto the shoe and you're ready to go.

If I'd invented Beanie Babies instead of taking up writing, I'd *own* this newspaper now instead of scratching out a column for it every two weeks.

Product packaging got worse in the '90's. I open up my 100% Bran cereal box to find it only half full. I wish the manufacturers would put it in a smaller box and pass the cardboard savings on to me.

This year I bought a 1998 Chevy Lumina, and then realized that it doesn't have any bumpers. Have we gotten so good at parallel parking in the '90's that bumpers aren't necessary anymore? Auto Club lobbyists must have ramrodded that idiotic design through so people can't go around pushing each other's cars to get them started.

There were some good movies in the '90's—"Schindler's List," "Good Will Hunting," "Nobody's Fool," and "Silence of the Lambs," to name a few. The worst movie of the decade had to be "Wayne's World." The second worst movie was "Wayne's World 2." Unfortunately, these two grossed more money than many of the good movies.

Speaking of making money in the 1990's, I think Elvis made more dead than alive. There are rumors afoot that the IRS is calling him in for an audit.

The 1990's saw common everyday items go hi-tech electronic, like telephones, gas pumps, car washes, bathroom scales, and the like. Is this progress? Try handing a young clerk a twenty-dollar bill for a purchase of $12.82, then just after he's pressed the buttons on the electronic cash register you say, "Here's two pennies." The computerized cash register has already calculated the change for the twenty, and the clerk, who hasn't had much practice adding numbers because it's not necessary anymore, doesn't know how to handle your two pennies. He's tempted to call the police and have you run in as a troublemaker.

This was the decade when companies quit using humans to answer telephones, handing the job over to sophisticated computing equipment optimally designed to drive customers crazy with a lengthy series of menu selections. Pretty soon these hi-tech answering machines will began closing business deals between themselves, ultimately overthrowing the humans in upper management who had them installed in the first place.

All kidding aside, it was a fine decade for me. My personal highlight was returning to Upper Michigan to live. I've made many new friends, met a lot of my readers, and travelled this wonderful peninsula from one end to the other.

A TINY TOT CHRISTMAS

A basic rule of life that has served me well in adulthood has been to never get near small children. Often, of course, it can't be helped, as when I'm travelling on an airplane. Tiny demons run and scream up and down the aisle, doing excellent impersonations of Near East hijackers. When that happens I'm always comforted with the thought that when the plane lands and we all disembark, I don't have to take these pint-sized terrorists with me. So when my cousin Karen, who annually invites me down for a Texas Christmas with her family, called and told me that her three-year-old granddaughter was going to be there also, I said, "What? You expect me—mortal enemy of little people—to rub elbows with a three-year-old for several days? Not on your life, Grandma!"

But I went down to Texas anyway, taking the precaution of renting a hotel room far enough away from Karen's house to guard against a child-induced nervous breakdown.

Two days before Christmas the initial confrontation took place at Karen's home. Jourdan, a three-foot-high, hazel-eyed pixie with—I was to find out later—an IQ of 280 and the endurance of an Olympic decathlon athlete, looked at me solemnly and said, "Huh ah, Onka Airee."

I turned to Kara, Karen's daughter and guardian-in-charge of three-year-olds, saying, "I didn't quite catch that."

"Jourdan said, 'Hello, Uncle Jerry,'" Kara replied.

Conversing with three-year-olds requires bilingual skills.

Grandma Karen and Grandpa Ron have five dogs which Jourdan thought were neat play toys. The older dogs wisely kept their distance, but the cocker spaniel puppy, totally ignorant of children, joyfully bounded up to the three-year-old on their first meeting. Sweet little Jourdan immediately threw a tight headlock on the puppy, bulging its eyes, and then did her best to bite the puppy's ear off.

At the dinner table that evening I nervously watched as Jourdan demonstrated her newly acquired skill with eating utensils. She had definitely mastered the art of stabbing food with a fork, yet many of the morsels got lost on the way to her mouth. The dogs immediately picked up the scent of meat and mashed potatoes on the dining-room carpet and made a mad dash to see who could scarf up the most dropped food.

When Kara at last determined that the little one had gotten enough food into her mouth to sustain life, Jourdan was rewarded with a holiday treat of a sack of baby marshmallows. She wiped her mouth with the edge of grandma's lace tablecloth, grabbed the marshmallows, and dashed out of the dining room, only to return a short time later without them.

"What did you do with your marshmallows?" Kara asked.

Jourdan gave her the blank look that small children reserve for exasperating adults.

"Go and find those marshmallows and bring them right here," Kara directed, knowing full well that rogue marshmallows in a house full of expensive carpeting, drapes, and furnishings represented a full-fledged crisis. "Move!" Kara snapped.

Jourdan dashed over to the puppy's food dish where she had

deposited the marshmallows as a peace offering for the headlock she'd earlier put on the little dog. She scooped up a handful of the marshmallows along with a generous helping of doggie kibble and jammed the mixture into her mouth, savoring it with much more enthusiasm than she'd had for the turkey and mashed potatoes served at the dinner table. The puppy was glad to see the food dish emptied because the marshmallows had been gluing her teeth together.

The next day we had to take Jourdan to Wal-Mart on a subversive mission to be sure that Santa was going to deliver the right size bicycle. The child proved to be an unsuspecting but enthusiastic accomplice by climbing aboard every new bike in the toy department. Grandma Karen finally steered her onto the only one that looked to be the right size. Before anyone could react, the little one began furiously pedalling it down the aisle, and although the bike had training wheels, it tipped over with a resounding crash. Kara dusted Jourdan off and said in a soothing voice, "But that's a nice bicycle anyway, don't you think?"

Jourdan eyed the bicycle with deep suspicion and said, "No!"

Grandma Karen rolled her eyes and handed me the keys to her car, whispering, "It's too late to change Santa's list now. While we're doing other shopping you sneak the bicycle into the sleigh."

I carried out the mission without a hitch, and when Christmas Day arrived, Santa delivered the bicycle right on schedule. In a matter of minutes Jourdan was zooming up and down the driveway like a Grand Prix cyclist. I'd hate to admit how long it took me to learn how to ride a bicycle.

Spending time with a three-year-old turned out to be an enlightening, even enjoyable experience. (I will never make this confession again.) Jourdan and I fed stale bread to the quack-quacks (ducks to those of you who don't speak Three-year-old), sculpted jolly snowmen out of Play Doh, and ate up an incredible tonnage of Christmas goodies. On our last day together we were getting into Grandma Karen's car to embark on a Day-After-Christmas-Sale shopping trip. This, I might add, is an extremely foolhardy endeavor for an inexperienced man.

"Mall!" yelled Jourdan as she was being strapped into her car seat.

Small girl children don't say "Mama" anymore.

MEMORIES OF WINTER

At this time of year it seems appropriate to share a few deep-freeze memories of winters past. Caution: if you don't like U.P. winters, don't read any further.

I was only five years old when the legendary Blizzard of 1938 came roaring through the U.P. While it was shaking the bejeezuz out of our drafty old wood-frame house in Ishpeming, I pleaded with my mother to dress me up in my woolen snowsuit (with attached mittens, of course) so I could dash outside and watch the blizzard up close. She looked at me like I'd lost my mind. I was told to keep quiet and go and sit next to the living-room wood stove.

The blizzard raged and howled throughout the day until the snow began piling up over the first-floor windows, and then the house got real quiet. By the next morning we couldn't hear a thing. Upstairs, daylight filtered through the ice-encrusted bedroom windows, but downstairs it was completely dark. My father tried to push open the outside door of the storm porch but got it open only a crack. All we could see through the crack was snow from floor to ceiling. We were literally buried in snow. The old man began battering his shoulder against the door, trying to force it open. He kept at it until the door was halfway open, but we still couldn't see daylight. Then he attacked it with a snow shovel that he'd had the foresight to keep in the kitchen. He finally poked through the snow that had drifted up against the house and for the rest of the day hacked a deep trench out to the street. It was never clear to me why he did that, because it would be two days before a plow could open up our street. Our backyard woodshed was completely buried. I remember asking the old man where the shed was and he said, "It's still out there . . . somewhere."

A few days later we were finally able to hike over to Division Street. It didn't look at all like downtown Ishpeming. The streets were deep snow-walled canyons with only the tops of the two-story buildings visible. Many people had hiked downtown on snowshoes to get groceries.

In those days there were no nighttime restrictions on street parking, and before the blizzard hit, many off-shift miners had driven downtown for a few quick ones, parking their cars on the streets next to the Ishpeming bars. The storm had trapped them inside their favorite watering holes, and they'd had to spend the night with nothing but dozens of liquor bottles to keep them company. I suppose that wasn't all that bad, but the next day, hungover, they had no idea which one of the ten-foot snow drifts along the streets contained their cars. A week later some of them were still tentatively poking the drifts with shovels, hoping to locate their frozen autos.

The coldest winter that I can remember was in 1949 and '50 when I was in high school and we were living in Republic on the Michigamme River. During the day it rarely got above zero, and every night it would regularly plunge to twenty or thirty below. Just before bedtime, my father would feverishly stoke up the kitchen and living room wood stoves until the temperature inside the house soared to eighty degrees. Then we'd hop into bed, clad in long underwear and sweaters, because after the fires died down the inside temperature would plummet.

The house didn't have an inside toilet, and only a fool would have ventured out to the privy perched on the river's edge with the butt-freezing wind whistling up through the two holes. So we used chamber pots, and I kept mine handy underneath the bed. One particular morning when I woke up I knew it was colder than usual. The contents of the chamber pot were frozen.

I jumped out of bed and into my woolen shirt and pants. The old man was up already, lighting fires in the two stoves and generally puttering around. He went out the back door and immediately called to me, "C'mon out here, ya gotta see this!"

I went out the back door, and he pointed triumphantly at the thermometer nailed to the door jamb. "Lookit that! Fifty-five below zero!" The old man was a weather buff, collecting record temperatures. Fifty-five below zero was going into his record book.

I made the mistake of taking a breath. The air was so cold that it felt hot, searing down my throat like a hot poker. My nose and ears immediately went numb. I ran back inside.

But after I recovered I got excited thinking about what a neat thing it would be to try to get my Model A Ford started. No one would want to walk around in weather like that, and I could drive into town and easily pick up girls, my number-one priority at the time.

It was going to require a lot of work, however. The car was sitting in the backyard with an empty radiator and no battery. I couldn't afford antifreeze to fill the radiator, so whenever I ran the car I used water spiked with just enough alcohol to get by. This worked fine except that the mixture would freeze at about ten below zero, so at night I'd have to drain the stuff into quart milk bottles and keep it in my bedroom. The battery was also in no shape to be left in the car in those temperatures, so I kept it under my bed next to the chamber pot.

I bundled up good with only my eyes exposed to the elements and lugged the car battery down to the Shell station and had a cheap quick charge put on it. Then I carried it back home, put it in the Model A, and filled up the radiator.

I grasped the engine crank in my leather choppers, inserted it into the crank hole beneath the radiator, and tried to turn the engine over. The crank didn't budge, not even a quarter turn. The motor oil was frozen solid. After a few minutes of that I had to give up and quickly drain my lean mixture of alcohol and water from the radiator before it froze too. Two days later, when it warmed up to a balmy ten below zero, I finally got the car running, but by then it was too late. The Republic girls preferred walking in ten-below-zero weather to riding around with me in my drafty Model A. I never did have much luck with women back in those days.

CAN YOU TOP THIS?

I'm sure that all of you, at one time or another, have done something pretty stupid, but can you top this?

I recently returned from a long weekend in Southern California, the land where millions of sun-soaked sufferers endure daily wind chill factors of seventy-five degrees above zero. Upon returning to Michigan I was gratified to find that the weather was a bit more invigorating as I landed at Sawyer International Airport at 8 PM on Monday. The wind-chill factor was well *below* zero and the fluffy white stuff was hurtling in horizontally. However, being an old systems engineer, I'd cleverly anticipated such an event and had parked my car close to the front entrance of the Sawyer terminal building as I departed for California. I'd worn my heavy winter coat onto the airplane and my cap and scarf were conveniently packed in an outside pocket of my suitcase which was scheduled to arrive at the baggage claim minutes after we touched down.

After I got inside the terminal there seemed to be a delay with the luggage, so I dashed out to my Chevy and drove it up to the front entrance. After pushing the LOCK/UNLOCK button on the inside of the driver's door to open the rear door to get my windshield snow scraper, I got out, slammed the driver's door, and tried to open the rear door.

Uh-oh. I'd pushed the button the wrong way and locked myself out of the car with the engine running.

I uttered a few well-chosen R-rated words and then went back inside the terminal and asked the people at the rental-car counters if they had any GM master keys. They had none.

I went over to Baggage Claim to retrieve my suitcase. It wasn't there. The suitcase hadn't come in on the same plane that I did.

The terminal was now emptying rapidly, but I noticed a forlorn-looking woman standing alongside at Baggage-Claim.

"Your luggage didn't arrive either?" I asked. She shook her head sadly. Sonia Archambeau had just returned from New Orleans, and she'd intended to change into her winter clothing in the terminal. However, they were packed in her suitcase which was cavorting with mine somewhere out there in the snow-filled boonies between the Minneapolis and Sawyer airports. Now kindred spirits, we went to the Northwest counter and inquired about our lost luggage.

"I can check on the whereabouts of your suitcases right now," the Northwest lady said helpfully. "Just give me the number on your baggage-claim tickets."

I explained that my claim ticket was in my carry-on case in the car and told her what had happened.

"You locked yourself out of your car with the engine running?" she said, suppressing a giggle, not believing that a person could possibly do anything that boneheaded. She then suggested that I phone the Sawyer security patrol, who were reportedly adept at dealing with this kind of problem. I called them, and a patrolman said that he'd be at the terminal within fifteen minutes.

Sonia had her pickup truck in the airport lot, and she graciously volunteered to wait around and drive me to Marquette to get a spare car key if the Sawyer patrolman wasn't able to unlock my Chevy. It was now going on 9 PM, and we were both getting hungry. I volunteered to spring for food. However, if you're stuck at the Sawyer terminal after the sun goes down, don't even think about coffee and sandwiches because there aren't any. Two vending machines dispense candy bars and soda for a dollar bill. Sonia just wanted some bottled water. I reached for my wallet, but all I had were fives and twenties. The machine wouldn't make change.

The security man finally arrived and took a look at my locked Chevy as it was happily idling its tankful of gas into the cold night air. "What year is this car?" he asked me.

"It's a '98."

He shook his head. "Can't touch it. I thought I might be able to use a Slim Jim, a wire that slips into the window well and trips the door lock, but if I stick the wire in there it, could set off the air bags. We can't be responsible. Sorry."

It was time to head for Marquette for my spare keys. Sonia handed me the key to her pickup. "Would you go and get my truck?" All she had on her feet were low-heeled shoes.

Out in the airport parking lot, Sonia's S-10 pickup had collected a knee-deep snow drift against the driver's side, but I resolutely waded through it and opened the door. The driver's seat was pushed all the way forward, and there was so much stuff jammed behind the seat that it wouldn't move back—I couldn't get behind the wheel. After a lot of grunting and cursing, I finally squeezed my butt into the driver's seat, and with my knees crammed up around my chin, I managed to get the truck over to the terminal entrance.

Sonia got behind the wheel and we took off, but the fun was just beginning. By now the snow on the Sawyer roadways was spin-your-wheels deep, and the stingy little signs directing you in and out of the airport were invisible in the flying snow. At one point we took a wrong turn and an airplane loomed up in the truck's windshield.

My gawd, I thought, we're on the airport runway! But it was only an old museum-piece jet fighter parked next to Voodoo Avenue. I think that the county should provide a regularly scheduled airport shuttle service, especially for winter air travellers. A half-track equipped with a GPS navigation system would be good.

We finally made it out to the highway and headed toward town. Thanks to Sonia and my kind landlady, Phyllis, who took me back to the airport, I finally got my car home before the stroke of midnight. I will never let this happen again. I'm going with the latest fashion trend: an earring just like the young guys, except mine's going to have a spare car key on it.

THE GREEN LANTERN BATTLES
THE NICKEL HAMBURGER

Whenever I go to Ishpeming I usually have lunch at Peggy Sue's Cafe with my long-time crony, Jeff Jacobs. Peggy Sue's has excellent food; my favorite is the meat-loaf sandwich and pea soup special for $4.50. I'll never forget the first time Jeff and I went out for lunch in Ishpeming. That was long ago when lunch cost a whole lot less.

Some background first. In 1941, superhero comic books were making the scene and fast becoming the rage among kids. *Action Comics* featuring Superman had been around for a couple of years, quickly followed by Batman, Captain Marvel, and The Flash. Captain America arrived on the scene in the spring of '41 and was busily bashing Hitler many months before the United States entered the war.

The trouble with comic books was that they cost ten cents, a fortune for kids in 1941. This exorbitant price spawned a lively business in comic-book trading. Every Saturday morning all other kid activities were suspended while we lugged large stacks of dog-eared comic books to each other's houses in the hope of finding the odd issue that we hadn't read.

However, sooner or later we had to buy new ones, and one day that summer I noticed the latest issue of *DC Comics* for sale in Newberry's on Main Street. *DC Comics* was my absolute favorite because it featured the Green Lantern, a real stand-up superhero. I could identify with the Green Lantern because he possessed only limited magical powers and would actually bleed whenever he got shot, which seemed to be often. I had to have that comic book, but I didn't have the ten cents.

I conferred with Kippy (Jeff's nickname when he was a kid) on what to do. We considered skulking into Newberry's, grabbing the *DC Comics* out of the rack, and making a run for it, but the Newberry's clerks were teenagers and pretty fast on their feet. The only other solution was to try to get the dime out of my father.

Prying money out of the old man was always a gruelling task because he had to have complete details on how you were going to spend it. I had to explain to him who the Green Lantern was, what he did for a living, and why he was deserving enough to warrant ten cents of the old man's money. My father finally gave in, mainly because he himself was addicted to *True Detective Magazine* which was at the same high-caliber literary level as *DC Comics*. I raced across the LS&I railroad tracks over to Kippy's house to tell him the good news, and we both headed off for downtown Ishpeming to make the purchase.

On the way to Newberry's we had to pass The Coffee Pot on First Street. The Coffee Pot was nothing but a tiny six-stool diner, but the place had one exotic feature. Above the door was an exhaust fan that sucked the smoke from the cook's grill and blew it out onto the street. Many a time I would stop on the sidewalk at The Coffee Pot just to breathe in the rich aroma of frying hamburgers on the grill. I was eight years old, and I'd never had a hamburger in my life. Sandwiches at my house were either baloney or peanut butter and jelly, and that was it. My lifelong dream then was to go into the Mather Inn dining room and order a hamburger.

As Kippy and I stood there, inhaling the overwhelmingly delicious fumes from The Coffee Pot's grill, I must have blacked out because the next thing I knew Kippy and I were inside the diner, sitting at the counter.

"Whadda you kids want?" the counterman asked.

"How much are your hamburgers?" I inquired.

"Five cents."

I carefully placed my dime on the counter. "Two hamburgers please." Just like that, my superhero, the Green Lantern, had battled the nickel hamburger and lost.

The counterman slapped two hamburger patties on the grill. The grease bubbled and spattered invitingly. "Whaddaya want on 'em?" he asked.

Kippy and I looked at him stupidly. Neither of us knew what he meant.

"Ya want onions, pickles, relish, sliced tomatoes, a li'l lettuce, what?"

"Put it all on," Kippy said decisively. I nodded in agreement.

The hamburgers were placed in front of us, staggering under their own weight. After slathering on catsup and mustard, we began to eat, hardly being able to get our kid-size mouths around the hamburgers. Somehow we managed though, and they were delicious.

On the way home, our stomachs pooching out, the realization hit me that I just might have a little trouble with the old man. I was right.

"Ya spent the dime on hamburgers?" he exclaimed, not believing his ears. Keeping the household supplied with food had been a fierce point of pride with my father during the Depression, and he didn't want any damn-fool kid of his blowing good money on hamburgers.

"Next time you get hungry, you come *home* to eat," he growled, then closed the discussion with a final parting shot. "An' don't ask me fer any more dimes! You kin just read yer old comic books over again."

And that's what I had to do. It would be long, long time before a new comic book found its way into our house.

I lost track of the Green Lantern shortly after that, but I understand that he was around fighting crime for several years. He couldn't have been the same old superhero though, after he lost the battle with the nickel hamburger.

DOWN AND OUT IN GREEN BAY

I hadn't had a regular eye exam in four years and figured that it was about time, so in January I went to visit an ophthalmologist in Marquette.

"You have ectropion of the lower lids," the doctor announced.

"What's that?" I asked fearfully.

"Droopy eyelids," he replied.

Well, I already *knew* that. I'd been looking at them in the mirror every morning for years, ugly as hell. Additionally, the lower lids drooped so much that I had to regularly use artificial tears to keep my eyes from drying out.

The ophthalmologist continued. "Dr. Dale in Green Bay specializes in reconstructive eye surgery. He can correct this condition."

I met with Dr. Dale two weeks later, and he explained the procedure. The surgery, he said, would entail horizontal tightening in addition to placement of an alloderm graft. In plain English, he would pull the muscle below the eye off to one side, tack it down with stitches, and then insert a piece of skin below the eye to prop up the lower lid. And are you ready for this? The skin segment comes from a cadaver so I wouldn't be inconvenienced by having them yank it off of me. Neat, eh?

I checked into the Bay Care Surgery Center in Green Bay to have the first eye done. I was apprehensive about the operation, but Dr. Dale's friendly staff immediately put me at ease. And the friendly stuff that they dripped into my vein before the surgery also helped a great deal.

In fact, the whole operation was a barrel of laughs. I was conscious but feeling no pain, and I joked with Dr. Dale as he sliced away. I didn't even mind when he looped a piece of surgical thread through my lower eyelid, pulled the lid up over my eyeball, and taped the ends of the thread to my forehead (I'm not making this up).

Still in a state of euphoria, I caught a cab back to my hotel. That's when the fun began. After the anesthetic wore off I found that not only was I totally blind in the eye that was sewn shut but that the other one was actually weeping in sympathy. I could barely see. I couldn't read or watch TV, in fact, getting to the bathroom was a challenge. But no time to just lie around and recover. Dr. Dale's final instructions were to apply an ice pack to the eye for five minutes, take it off for five minutes and then ice it again, keeping this up for forty-eight hours. Ice packs every five minutes for *two days*? Have these doctors ever tried to follow their own instructions?

I stumbled down the hallway, looking for the ice machine, only to find that it was broken. I had to journey up one floor to get ice. The ice was the crushed variety that melts immediately, so I spent the rest of the day and evening groping my way up to the next floor to fill my ice bucket. On one such trip as I waited for the elevator, the door opened and a woman began to emerge. She took one look at me, jumped back, and unsuccessfully attempted to stifle a scream. Who could blame her? Can you imagine stepping out of an elevator and being confronted by an angry bearded man with a lower eyelid tacked to his forehead?

I'd come to Green Bay alone, figuring that with one good eye I could easily drive home the day after surgery. But with the shape that both of my eyes were in, there was no way I was going to be able to drive back to Marquette, or even around the block for that matter. I didn't know anyone in Green Bay, so I could be stuck in the hotel for days. What was I going to eat? The hotel had complimentary breakfasts but nothing else. There wasn't a restaurant within walking distance, and I wasn't too swift at walking anyway.

The situation was indeed serious, and I decided to call someone in the U.P. to come down to get me. I knew that my friend Jeff would have done it, but he was recovering from a hernia operation and wasn't up to driving. My cousin Barb had her ankle in a cast. Furthermore, I would have to find two people, one to drive my car back and one to drive their's back. This shortened the list of possible candidates considerably, but I began making calls.

A credit-card call from a hotel room requires punching in thirty-seven numbers, which is not easy when the telephone is a blur. After finally managing to get the numbers right I discovered that no one on my list was home. I was marooned in Green Bay, Wisconsin, doomed to blindness and starvation. I took two Extra Strength Tylenol and went to bed.

The following morning I ate breakfast at the hotel, slowly and carefully steering each spoonful of Cheerios toward my mouth. Then I took a cab to the doctor's office for a post-op appointment. En route I suddenly realized that my good eye wasn't tearing anymore. I could actually see, albeit with only one eye.

"That eye looks fine," Dr. Dale said cheerfully, referring to the one that he had carved on the day before.

"Quit the kidding," I said. "I saw it in the mirror this morning."

"No, really, it's doing great."

"I'm going to try to drive back to Marquette today," I told him.

"Well, good luck," he said. Dr. Dale is a surgeon, not a traffic-safety advisor.

Twenty miles north of Green Bay I ran into dense fog on US-41 and had to slow down to thirty-five miles an hour, although with only one good eye I wasn't really up to going much faster anyway. In Marinette I stopped for lunch and scared the bejeezuz out of a SUBWAY clerk when I entered the restaurant. Being ugly is no fun.

After four hours of labored one-eyed driving I finally pulled into my driveway. The really depressing aspect is that later this month I get to do it all over again with the other eye. I'll keep you posted.

KING KONG WHEELS

One day in 1971, while I was still living in California, I bought a brand-new Chevrolet pickup truck. I brought it home and my wife yelled, "You spent three thousand dollars on a *TRUCK*?" We got divorced shortly after that. I got the pickup in the settlement, not a bad deal considering that I kept it until 1999, certainly outlasting the furniture that my ex-wife was awarded.

My twenty-nine-year relationship with the '71 Chevy left me with a lasting emotional bond with pickup trucks; I just flat out like them. I don't own one now since the only stuff I have to haul are groceries from Jack's IGA, but still, old loves die hard, so when my friend Jeff and I were walking around the Auto Show at the Superior Dome a few weeks ago, a new pickup was in the back of my mind.

As usual Jeff wanted to look over the new Cadillacs, since the miles continue to pile up on the one that he has. (The Caddy has nineteen thousand on it.) But there were no Cadillacs in the Auto Show this year, not enough room apparently. The pickup trucks and SUV's were taking up all of the floor space, not because there were so many of them, but because they were so big. Have you seen the size of these things? The tops of the wheels come up to your chin. You need a stepladder to clean the windshield. Running boards are making a comeback because you can't get into these vehicles without them. I tried climbing into a new Dodge Ram without running boards and almost split the seat of my pants. If your wife is wearing a tight skirt, you'll need a forklift to get her into one of these new trucks.

And it's not only size, it's power. For many years four-cylinder engines in pickups were commonplace. Well, guess what? Now you can get V-10 engines. I suppose a V-10 would come in handy if you get into a drag race while hauling your boat to the lake, but I personally don't think I'd be able to put up with the loud slurping sound coming from beneath the hood. With a V-10 you won't find gas-mileage estimates on the window sticker (it's not required for anything bigger than a V-8) which means you'd have to take out a second mortgage on the old homestead to drive to Green Bay.

Jeff and I were chuckling at the absurdity of these big hulks, and I'd about kissed off the idea of buying a new pickup as being totally impractical. Then we drifted over to the Ford display area. There on the floor, casting a long shadow across the length of the Dome, was a Ford F-350. The others were big, but they were sardine-can compacts compared to the 350. I couldn't believe it. I was looking at the King Kong of pickup trucks. The four-door crew cab had more room inside than some apartments I've lived in. The truck bed was big enough to hold my Oldsmobile in case I wanted to carry it along as a spare.

Intrigued, I climbed up onto the leather captain's seat. Above my head, like an Apollo spacecraft, was a bank of switches, no doubt for activating an electric tailgate and special navigational lights needed on a vehicle of this size. I stared out of the massive windshield at the people on the floor, scurrying around below me like little ants. I cackled with glee. It was like being King of the Mountain.

I carefully climbed down to check out the engine as all guys are expected to do. With considerable effort I lifted the huge hood, but then a hidden counterweight system took over and it rose on its own, soaring far above my reach.

Looking under the hood I nodded sagely like I knew exactly what I was doing. I couldn't even *see* the big engine, but I supposed it was down there somewhere, lurking beneath the large number of fluid reservoirs, black boxes, and sixteen miles of weird wiring and plumbing.

I was covetously running my fingers along the mile-long length of the monster's side when a Ford salesperson appeared out of nowhere, all smiles. "This baby has a one-hundred-and-seventy-two-inch wheelbase," he exclaimed proudly.

I did the math in my head. "Over fourteen feet?"

"That's longer than your best ski jump when you were a kid," Jeff said.

"Where would you *park* something this big?" I asked.

"Anywhere you want," Jeff replied. The salesman nodded in agreement.

That's right, I thought. After all, I'd have the biggest pickup truck in town. I COULD park it anywhere I want! My hands were getting sweaty, a common reaction when a Yooper looks at a new pickup. I realized that buying this megaton of portable iron would be total madness, but I began thinking of reasons why I really needed it. With that wheelbase I'd never have to worry about falling into a Michigan pothole. I could buy two-years worth of groceries and easily get them home in one trip.

"I've got to get out of here," I muttered to Jeff. "My hand is starting to reach for my credit card."

Jeff was no help. "There's a desk over there where you can sit down and work out a deal."

With considerable effort I shakily made it out the door without doing anything foolish. "Whew, that was close," I said to Jeff. "Why didn't you remind me that I don't need a pickup truck any more?"

Jeff gave me a sly grin. "The Auto Show is still open tomorrow if you wanna come back and take another look."

"No, I think I'd better seek professional help," I said.

A CAMP STORY

I t's that time of year again when every red-blooded Yooper is thinking about opening up his camp for the summer season. It's been a good many years since I've had a camp, but I still remember the thrill and pride of ownership.

In 1946, at age thirteen, I was spending the summer with my grandparents in Republic. My pal, Glenn Brown, and I were totally immersed in a highly technical project—we were building a shotgun. In my grandfather's woodshed I'd discovered a piece of water pipe with an inside diameter to perfectly accommodate a .410 shotgun shell. We took a hack saw and cut the pipe to the proper length for the gun barrel. This would be a highly unorthodox shotgun with a barrel of galvanized iron instead of tempered steel, but Glenn and I were not adverse to taking risks.

We were filing off the rough edges from the end of the pipe when my Uncle Arvid stopped by and asked us what we were doing. I told him. Arvid didn't say anything right then, but he came back later, obviously concerned that we might actually find a way to fire the kludged-up weapon. He had come up with an alternative idea to divert our energies.

"How'd you kids like a camp? I got one you can have."

Of course we thought he was joking. No one gives a camp away. I chuckled at Arvid's humor and went back to carving our shotgun stock out of a two-by-four.

Arvid continued. "Th'camp's out east of town. All you gotta do is fix it up an' it's yours."

He finally convinced us that he wasn't kidding, so we followed him out of town, past the cemetary. After a half-mile trek along a winding footpath through the woods we came to the camp. It was a tiny log cabin—eight feet by eight feet—with barely enough headroom, even for us kids. Arvid had built it in the 1920's when he was a teenager, and it had been abandoned for many years. The door was hanging by one hinge and had been well chewed by resident porcupines. The tarpaper roof was in shreds. The only window had two broken panes. It was bare inside, except for a carpet of porcupine poop covering the splintery wooden floor. But it was ours, and Glenn and I quickly got enthused.

"It needs a li'l work," Arvid admitted. "But you got all summer."

Bright and early the next morning Glenn and I were at the Republic town dump near my grandmother's house. We were there to get furniture for our new camp. We didn't really have to search the dump because we already knew where everything was. Glenn and I were experts on the Republic town dump; we spent most of the daylight hours there. The dump satisfied our adolescent lust for setting fires, and the fires had the additional benefit of driving the rats out into the open, thus providing excellent BB-gun target practice. And, of course, any treasures one found in the dump were *absolutely free!* Glenn and I had already picked over the mountain of trash many times, so that morning we knew exactly where to go to find what we were after. There was a badly wrecked '36 Ford with serviceable seat cushions which would make two excellent camp beds. We pulled the seats out of the car and carried them, one by one, out to the camp.

Then we began working on the camp itself. We plugged up the chinks between the logs with tree moss. There was no money to buy new tarpaper, so we patched up the roof with old tarpaper scavenged from the dump. We found another hinge for the door and replaced the broken window panes with cardboard.

One day at the dump Glenn and I discovered the ultimate bonanza; someone had discarded a small potbellied stove. With shouts of glee we waded through the trash, picked up the stove, and headed for camp. The stove, though small, was cast iron and heavy as hell. I suspect that the herniated disk that I suffered with in 1999 was initially caused by lugging that cast iron stove a half mile through the woods.

Finally, after many days of hard work, the camp was ready. Glenn and I decided to give it the acid test: staying overnight. At home we filled potato sacks with pillows, blankets, candles, pans, canned goods, soda pop, white bread, peanut butter, Velveeta cheese, and Twinkies. It required two trips to lay in all of the supplies, but by late afternoon we were ready to relax and enjoy our new camp.

Then it began to rain. In no time at all it was pouring, and we quickly discovered that our roof repairs were somewhat less than satisfactory. In fact, the roof leaked like a sieve. Our two pans had to be pressed into service to catch the biggest leaks while we jockeyed the car-seat beds around the tiny floor space to minimize the amount of water dripping on them.

When darkness fell we lit a couple of candles and proceeded to build a fire in the stove. This should have been no problem whatsoever because, after all, who was more expert at lighting fires than Glenn and I? However, the stove pipe wasn't drawing too well. In fact, the camp began filling up with dense smoke, and we had to open the door and tear out the cardboard from the window to air the place out.

Now it was time to prepare the evening meal. The menu consisted of toasted-cheese sandwiches, pork and beans, cream soda, and

Twinkies. We planned to toast the sandwiches on the stove top, and that would have worked fine except for the roof leak right above the stove. While the underside of the sandwich was being toasted, the top side was getting saturated with dripping rainwater. When it was discovered that we'd forgotten to bring along forks and a can opener, I had to punch open the tops of the pork and bean cans with my trusty hunting knife.

We placed the food on our orange-crate table and began to eat. By some standards the meal may have left something to be desired—stove-blackened, soggy cheese sandwiches, pork and beans eaten out of the can with a hunting knife, lukewarm cream soda, and Twinkies. Ah, but it was delicious and we wolfed it all down.

There wasn't much to do after that, so we went to bed. Glenn and I lay on our wet car-seat beds under damp blankets, trying to ignore the rainwater plinking us in the ear. We looked at each other with smoke-reddened eyes and grinned.

What could possibly be any better than this?

BIOGRAPHY

Jerry Harju was born in Ishpeming, Michigan, in 1933. He received a degree in engineering mechanics from the University of Michigan in 1957 and a MS from the University of Southern California in 1985. After thirty years as a manager in the aerospace industry in Southern California, Jerry began writing as a second career. His first three books, *Northern Reflections, Northern D'Lights,* and *Northern Passages,* are collections of humorous short stories about his experiences while growing up in Michigan's Upper Peninsula in the 1940's. His fourth book, *The Class of '57,* takes readers along a humorous and nostalgic path during Harju's six years of "higher education" at the University of Michigan. University life then—with its 1950's attitudes on world affairs, morality, and women's roles in society—was much different from today. The fifth book, *Cold Cash,* is Jerry's first novel, a wacky tale about two heros, totally unschooled in criminal activity, who decide to solve their cash-flow problems by pulling a bank heist with a getaway on snowmobiles. Typical of Harju's work, the robbery doesn't go as planned and is further complicated by two strong-willed women.

Jerry Harju now lives in Marquette, Michigan, spending his time writing books and newspaper columns and travelling all over the globe.